# ANGLO-SAXON
# & NORMAN
# BRISTOL

# ANGLO-SAXON & NORMAN BRISTOL

*David*
*Sivier*

TEMPUS

*To my parents*

First published 2002

PUBLISHED IN THE UNITED KINGDOM BY:
Tempus Publishing Ltd
The Mill, Brimscombe Port
Stroud, Gloucestershire GL5 2QG
www.tempus-publishing.com

PUBLISHED IN THE UNITED STATES OF AMERICA BY:
Tempus Publishing Inc.
2A Cumberland Street
Charleston, SC 29401
www.tempuspublishing.com

British Library Cataloguing in Publication Data.
A catalogue record for this book is available from the British Library.

ISBN 0 7524 2533 1

Typesetting and origination by Tempus Publishing.
PRINTED AND BOUND IN GREAT BRITAIN.

# Contents

# Acknowledgements

During this book's long gestation I have become indebted to a multitude of people for their kind advice, encouragement and assistance, with sometimes original material. My thanks particularly to the Bristol Diocesan Board of Education for material on All Saints' Church; Canon John Rogan and the administrator of Bristol Cathedral, Mrs Joy Coupe; Jerry Baker of the Environment, Transport and Leisure Department, Bristol City Council; Sue Giles, curator of the numismatics collection, Bristol City Museum; Mr Lionel Reeves and the churchwardens of Westbury on Trym parish church; Miryam Clough, churchwarden of Horfield parish church; John Seeley, churchwarden of St Nicholas, Whitchurch, and Rev. James Wilson of the parish of Whitchurch. My thanks also to Prof. Philip Rahtz for allowing me to use figures **16**, **17**, **21**, **22**, **43**, **44**, **45**, and **46**, which first appeared in his Lorna Watts' book *St Mary le Port Bristol*, p.97, 96, 167, 142, 98, 99, 100, 135, 149, 148, 152, and 155, respectively; Dr Les Good of the City Museum archaeological department for figures **67** and **68**, which first appeared in his article *Some Aspects of the Development of the Redcliffe Waterfront in the light of Excavation at Dundas Wharf*, p 30 and 32; figures **24**, **27**, **28**, **32**, **34**, **37**, **38** and **39**, which appeared in *Bristol Castle Keep: A re-appraisal of the evidence and report on the excavations in 1989*, p.18, 22, 19, 21, 31, 34, and 36, and 37; and his permission to use figures **7**, **8** and **9** from P. Belsey's and M. Ponsford's *A Late Roman Buckle and Medieval Building at Stockwood, Bristol*, p.3 and 4; and also for allowing me to see the Anglo-Saxon remains from the Castle now kept at the Museum; Michael Ponsford for his advice regarding his excavation of the Castle site and for the use of the above illustrations on the Stockwood finds; Prof. Mick Aston for his help on Roman roads around Bristol and the use of figure **3** originally appearing in *Monasteies in the Landscape*, p.123; Prof. Julian Richards for his information on Viking age ships; David Hill on the earldoms of Anglo-Saxon England; James Russell, for allowing me to use figure **12**, from his paper *The Parish of Clifton*, p.139; and R.G.J. Williams for figure **13**, from his paper *Further Investigations at St John the Baptist Church, Bedminster*, p.28; and David Dawson, for allowing me to use Barbara Cumby's drawings for his paper, *Archaeology and the Medieval Churches of Bristol, Abbot's Leigh and Whitchurch*, p.10 and 11 for figures **40** and **41**. Also owed and given thanks for their help are Mr Kim Siddorn, National Co-ordinator of *Regia Anglorum*, Ben Francis, webmaster Chris Romer for scouring the electronic byways of the internet, and Norma Hill for reading through and offering kind comments on the manuscript. Throughout writing the book I've enjoyed the immense generosity and encouragement of all the above people, who showed themselves patient and eager to share their enthusiasm for this distant but fascinating epoch of the City's history. I hope it does both them and the City justice, and passes this interest on to the reader. If it does not, the fault is entirely mine.

*Wes thus hael!*

David Sivier
Bristol, 2002

# Introduction

This book is an attempt to describe the city of Bristol in all its aspects from its origins at the end of the tenth century, to the end of the Norman dynasty and the ascent of Henry Plantagenet to the English throne, examining not just its political institutions, but its industries, agriculture, buildings and everyday lives of its citizens. The task hasn't been an easy one: there have been many pitfalls to be surmounted.

The first is defining the limits of the city itself. Unlike that of its island home, Bristol's geography is always changing, expanding. From its core around modern Castle Park, Bristol has sprawled outwards in one direction to overrun Redcliffe, Totterdown, Bedminster, Hengrove, Hartcliffe, Knowle, Withywood, Whitchurch and Stockwood, which were mostly still outside the city as late as the end of the nineteenth century, and some portions of which are still beyond the formal boundaries, even after the construction of estates abutting them in the 1960s. In the opposite direction the city has absorbed Stokes Croft, Southmead, Henbury, Westbury on Trym, Brentry, Henleaze, Lockleaze, Clifton, Redland, Hotwells, and Eastville, quite apart from the city's medieval wards of St Werburgh's, St Paul's, and Montpellier. Some of these, like Mangotsfield, Clifton and Westbury on Trym, existed as far back as the eleventh century, and were even then being drawn into the city's political and economic orbit.

The historian is left with the problem of which to include and which to leave out. As this is a history of Bristol, rather than that of the former, unlamented County of Avon, I have concentrated on the historic site of Bristol as it was in the Anglo-Saxon and Norman period. Other places are mentioned as they appear in connection with Bristol, either as part of its manor, such as Barton Regis, part of which became Barton Hill, or because of a religious connection with the city, such as Westbury on Trym, or other economic links, such as Pucklechurch. It is tempting to include every settlement, hamlet and village now either absorbed or made a suburb of the city – they are somebody's historic home, after all. This has had to be resisted. There is the danger that too much of little relevance will be included, and that rather than illuminating the development of the town the book will get bogged down in the details of the surrounding settlements, turning it into little more than a reiteration and critique of *Domesday*. This would be quite tedious to write and equally tedious to read. There is always an arbitrary element in all this, and so I ask those citizens of parts of the city I may have missed out to bear with me.

Of more importance than this is the sheer lack of information about Bristol in this period. Perceptive readers will note the monotonous regularity with which phrases such as 'may have been', 'probably', and 'perhaps' appear, and the tentative nature of many of my conclusions. This is from necessity, not choice. Anglo-Saxon and Norman Bristol occupied what is now the city's financial and business district, the most heavily developed part of the city. This has limited archaeological investigation, which as a rule has been done only when the area was being redeveloped. In the case of St Mary le Port Street and College Green, this took place after bomb damage from the Second World War. There have been other digs, at Redcliffe, Bristol Bridge, Castle Park and Tower Lane, among others, but large sections of the city still await excavation.

These digs have yielded relatively few finds, certainly not comparable in number with the plethora of items recovered from Viking York, London and Dublin. They are, however, of interest and importance despite this. They still provide valuable information on the activities going on in the city, even if to get a proper idea of their true significance we have to look elsewhere. There are gaps in our knowledge. Much has not survived, so where information on certain aspects of Bristolian life is lacking, I have filled the gap by referring to those other towns where evidence has come down to us.

There is a similar lack of documentary evidence. Bristol does not appear in the *Burghal Hidage*, the main source of information on late Saxon towns. Domesday Book is slightly more forthcoming, but still does no more than hint at the town's true situation; and in many ways it raises more questions than it answers. Although the product of the first Norman king's need to itemize and control his new kingdom, Domesday also provides information on the state of English towns and villages during the reign of Edward the Confessor, and the infrastructure that made its execution possible was largely Anglo-Saxon. Things had changed and were still changing by the time the survey was compiled, but it still provides useful information on late Saxon society, even if it dates from 19 years after that society's demise. It is also one of the few documents that mentions Bristol.

Anglo-Saxon England lacks the wealth of material from Carolingian France, for example, where private landlords listed the types, rights and duties of their estates' tenants. Much of our information about their social structure and the lives of the manorial tenants comes from the *Rectitudines Singularum Personarum* and the *Tidenham Custumal*. Bristol is fortunate in that although some of the conditions described in these two documents were not universally applicable throughout the country, because they were based on the situation in two Gloucestershire estates they may not have been too different from matters prevailing in Bristol and Barton Regis.

Sometimes, to illustrate particular points about town and other aspects of Anglo-Saxon and Norman life, I have gone farther afield, beyond England to the continent. This is justified. In these days of Euroscepticism and debate over national identity in the new Europe, it is often forgotten that England has always been a member of an international community, even before its conquest by *Guillaume le Batard*. England was part of Christendom, the seamless robe of Christ, which stretched from Ireland across Europe to the Byzantine Empire and Constantinople. Nobles, prelates and some humbler people crossed regularly to the continent, often on pilgrimages to Rome. Kings were in regular contact with each other. An effective law in one country was likely to be copied by the rulers of another. In the world of art, subjects and style flowed from Britain to the Continent and back again. English art of the Winchester school is only truly comprehensible when seen as part of the European Christian artistic tradition, taking some of its conventions from places as far-flung as Carolingian France, Ireland, Italy and Byzantium, and the Norse countries. These influences percolated down to the local level, to influence the carvings and paintings which would have adorned Bristol's churches. National and regional differences were strong, but even then Europe was groping its way towards a common culture of religion, politics and social organization. Even costume and military equipment were roughly similar.

Any discussion of the Norman contribution to the city's architecture is complicated by the fact that the style of architecture to which they gave their name preceded the Norman dynasty by a century or so, and outlasted it by 46 years. Properly called Romanesque, the style first appeared in Italy in the tenth century. Although it was vastly expanded in England by the Normans, it had been introduced a generation earlier by Edward the Confessor, whose abbey at Westminster was the country's first great Romanesque foundation. Elements of Romanesque architecture also appeared elsewhere in the country, such as in the crossing piers of the church at Stow in Lincolnshire, and in Wulfric's abbey of St Augustine in Canterbury. The finest example of domestic Norman architecture in Bristol is the hall found under the site of the chapel of St Bartholomew's Hospital in Lewin's Mead, built around 1170, 16 years after the Norman dynasty itself had become extinct and when their architecture was just beginning to feel the first touches of the Gothic. It has, nevertheless, been included because it represents the culmination of the Norman architectural tradition in Bristol, and was built to house magnates whose power and influence had emerged under the preceding dynasty.

The conclusions drawn will always, like the preceding chapters, be tentative. There is still much to be excavated, much that yet remains to be discovered. With these caveats, however, a book on Anglo-Saxon and Norman Bristol can still be sensibly written, and a few firm conclusions drawn. Bristol's origins lie in the Anglo-Saxon period, and its industries and trading contacts influenced much of its subsequent history, even if the nature of Saxon Bristol still remains problematic. I hope that this book provides a reasonably accurate picture of the life of the town in the eleventh and twelfth centuries, and that it may stimulate some readers to look further into the fascinating world of Dark Age and Medieval Britain.

# 1 The site of Anglo-Saxon Bristol

The history of Anglo-Saxon Bristol is short; about 66 years, from its foundation around AD 1000 to the Norman Conquest of 1066. Nevertheless, this period is important, constituting as it did the city's vigorous infancy. The original settlement of *Bricg Stowe* 'the place of assembly by the bridge', was built on a promontory then formed by the Avon and its tributary, the Frome, before the latter was diverted in the twelfth century. Further south, beyond and to the west of the Avon, lay marshland, the memory of which is perpetuated in Canon's Marsh. It was thus a superbly defended site, with its bridge (assumed to be identical with Bristol Bridge) crossing the Avon at its lowest point. At this promontory's heart were Broad Street, High Street, Wine Street and Corn Street forming a grid pattern, although the settlement did stretch across what is now Castle Green, whose eponymous castle, erected by the Normans, guarded the eastern approaches to the city. Rubbish pits from the Saxon period have also been found at St Bartholomew's Hospital and Tower Lane, suggesting that the town extended north over the Frome to the bottom of Christmas Steps; and

**1** *The city's historic centre, Wine Street, Corn Street and Broad Street today*

13

**2** *The remains of St Peter's, Castle Park, showing north tower*

that this area is called Lewin's Mead again suggests an origin in the Anglo-Saxon period. It is possible, though unlikely, that it was named after Leofwine Godwinson, King Harold's brother; another possibility is that it was named after several men of the same name who were prominent locally during the twelfth century, such as Lewin, son of Aelfric, who owned property in the city; Lewin the Chamberlain, who witnessed several of the Earldom of Gloucester's charters in the mid-twelfth century; or even yet another leading twelfth-century citizen, Lewin Larus. It has been suggested that the timber buildings found on the east side of Castle Park with their residues of pottery and iron slag represent all that remains of an industrial suburb associated with the town. This notion is contradicted by other evidence coming from excavations at Tower Lane, where a quantity of pottery, animal bone and metal slag was also discovered at the west end of the site approaching Tailors Court and Broad Street, and further finds of late Saxon and Norman pottery from Cyder House Passage, between Broad Street and Tower Lane. This has also been taken as evidence of industrial activity, and so it seems unlikely that Bristol was planned according to notions of zoning various occupations.

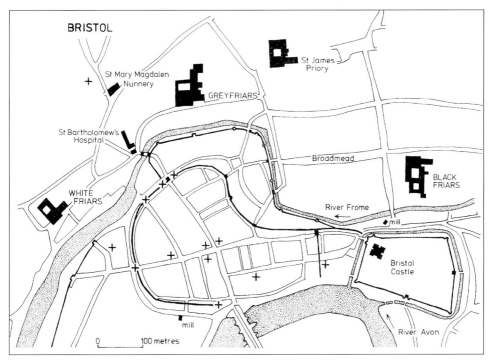

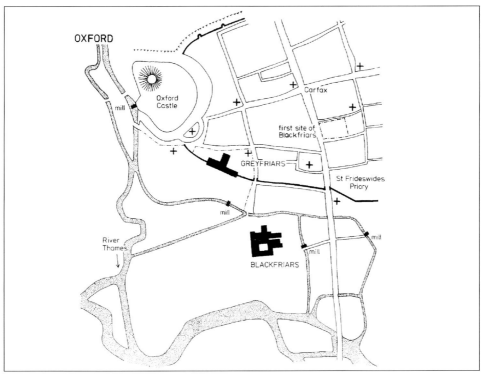

**3** *Plan of Anglo-Saxon and Norman Bristol with plan of Oxford for comparison.*
Courtesy of Mick Aston

**4** *City limits: St John's and the remains of the thirteenth-century city wall*

There may well have been buildings stretching over the whole of what is now Castle Park which have been destroyed, with the remains obliterated when the Castle was built. The dedication to St Werbergha indicates that her church may well have been founded before the Conquest, while the name of the now lost St Edith's Well, although first recorded much later, similarly suggests origins in the Anglo-Saxon period. The City's foremost church, St Peter in Peter Street, described in its 1105 confirmation to Tewkesbury Abbey as '*primitivum et principalem esse omnium ecclesiarum de Bristo*', was certainly founded during the Anglo-Saxon period, probably as the manor church of Barton Regis. It is probably St Peter's which the compilers of the *Domesday Book* described as 'the church' in Bristol. Aside from its leading role in the City, it was the mother church to those of Stapleton and Henbury.

Bristol Bridge may then have been further upstream than it is now, perhaps by about 70 or so yards, and there may have been a wharf area around it, bounded partly by St Mary le Port Street. The main thoroughfares and streets from Temple Meads line up in that direction, though these settlements date from the twelfth century, and so are really only suggestive. Furthermore, at its present site, the bridge would have made access to the city's harbour facilities difficult, as they were further upstream beyond the Bridge. This was obviously a disadvantage for shipping, though an obvious advantage in terms of defence: if the bridge did occupy its present site, it could defend the port's harbour from seaborne raiders coming from the estuary. There are strong arguments on both sides, and until further evidence is found, the matter must remain undecided. Aside from this, although the location of the Saxon quays is unknown, excavations at St Bartholomew's Hospital did uncover two possible wooden piers for a bridge over the Frome. In all, evidence from Bristol's Saxon period has come from nine sites covering an area 700 by 250m.

It appears that Bristol's grid layout was intentional. Its site and structure suggest it was built as a *burh*, a fortified town which acted as both a trading point and military stronghold constructed by the Anglo-Saxon monarchs in response to the Viking assaults. Although it is tempting to locate Bristol's foundation within the reigns of Edward the Elder and Aetheldreda, the Lady of the Mercians, sometime between 899-911, evidence for this is entirely lacking. Bristol is not mentioned in the *Burghal Hidage* of *c*.919, listing the *burhs* then extant in England, and the earliest dating evidence for the city is a coin of Aethelred II issued sometime between 1009-16. Despite this, the city was almost certainly in existence long before then. Its status as a *burh* is incontrovertible, however, given the strong similarities between the City and other late Saxon *burhs* mentioned in the *Burghal Hidage*. Like Bristol, a high percentage of the new settlements listed there (including Towcester in Northamptonshire, Twyneham in Dorset, Lydford in Devon, and Lyng and Lamport in Somerset) is situated on promontories in which the settlement is bounded on three sides with natural slopes or marshland, leaving only the promontory neck to be fortified. Like Bristol, many *burhs* were located close to Roman roads and the

**5** *Modern Broad Street, looking towards St John's*

**6** Sic transit gloria mundi: *the remains of Bristol Castle keep with St Peter's in the distance*

lowest bridging point of rivers. There was a Roman road running from Sea Mills to Bath, while the rivers Avon, Frome and Chew would also have formed important trade arteries allowing the trans-shipment of goods from the area around Bristol and Bath in the Roman period.

Excavations at Winchester, Wareham, Wallingford, Cricklade and elsewhere have shown that *burhs* were built on a grid pattern, after the model of the *insulae* tenement blocks in Roman cities, though not necessarily following the layout of their Roman predecessors, with back streets running parallel to the main street which were then intersected by other streets built at right angles to them, the whole area surrounded by a street running around the entire inner wall. From the evidence of Saxon and Norman archaeological sites and the description of the City's medieval topography preserved in William Worcestre's fifteenth-century account, it appears that Tower Lane was the intramural lane immediately behind the eastern City wall. The wall then looped north to run just within modern Nelson Street up to the churches of St John the Baptist, St Laurence and St Giles. From here the western wall, situated almost parallel to Small Street, curved round to St Leonard's Church, before roughly following the course of modern St Nicholas' Street to St Nicholas' Church. The siting of these churches on the wall may not be accidental. Although the churches of St John, St Leonard and St Nicholas were founded *c*.1100, with St Lawrence and St Giles constructed rather later (possibly in the twelfth and thirteenth centuries respectively), their positions over the City gates may ultimately derive from Saxon predecessors, as has been found elsewhere in the country. Even without St Werburgh's suggestive name, its location along with the churches of Christchurch and St Ewen's at the City's central crossroads seems to indicate that they date from the City's foundation, occupying as they do prime sites which would otherwise have been quickly subdivided.

The eastern part of the *burh*'s boundary is unclear. It may have been the 1.5m-deep trench excavated at the eastern end of St Mary le Port Street. It

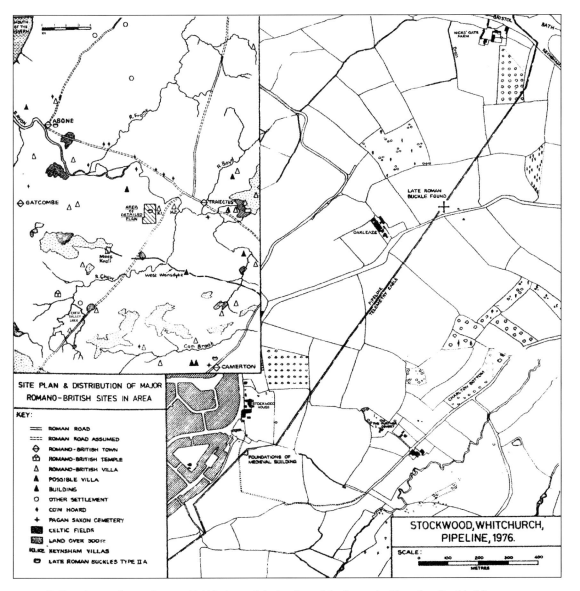

**7** *Distribution of major Romano-British sites and the locations of the Roman buckle and medieval buildings at Stockwood.* Courtesy of Les Good

could also have been Dolphin Street, known prior to its widening in 1770 as Defence Street. This may refer either to its role in the 'Burgesses' Revolt' of 1312, or retain a memory of its earlier function as the *burh*'s eastern intramural lane, with Worshipfull Street performing this function on the river side. The name of this latter street perhaps gives some clue to the location of the original bridge. Lying between the now destroyed St Mary le Port Street and the Avon, Worshipfull, or Worship Street was destroyed in 1766 by the redevelopment of Bridge Street, now, like its predecessor, destroyed in its turn.

Worship Street appears to be a corruption of *Worcheschepe*, itself a mid-fourteenth-century corruption of the earlier *wortheslupe*, meaning wharf-slipway. The earliest surviving form of the street's name is *w(o)rteslippestret*, from about 1180, which pre-dates the movements of the quays in the thirteenth century, and suggests the location of the original harbour during the Anglo-Saxon and Norman periods. It has, however, also been suggested that the first element in the name is not *waroth*, a wharf, but *worth*, an enclosure, in which case the street preserved the southern boundary of an enclosure discovered under St Mary le Port during the excavations of 1963. Moreover, excavation of Church Street near St Peter's not only yielded the early twelfth-century town wall, but also fragments of Saxo-Norman pottery, indicating a possible origin in the eleventh century for this street as well.

The street grid may also have included a road running from the pre-1960s western end of Castle Park eastwards along a medieval road enclosed within the castle bounds, and a parallel street roughly located on the present Castle Street further south, the eastern end of which met Old Market and might have formed the *burh*'s eastern gate. Alternatively, it is possible that the grid pattern was devised by the Normans when Geoffrey of Coutances began building the castle on the eastern part of the settlement, thus forcing the population to move westwards. There are, however, possible remains of a grid pattern in the Saxon buildings under the castle site, as well as suggestive parallels between Bristol and South Cadbury, hinting that the Norman castle's earthworks and early east gate may well have been part of the late Saxon town, as an intentional, integral part of its plan or as an early extension. Other areas in which the Normans placed their new castles on top of pre-existing Saxon fortifications include Castle Neroche in Somerset, Castle Bromwich in the West Midlands and at Chalgrave in Bedfordshire, in which, like Bristol, remains of a timber building were discovered under the Norman *motte*, though it is unclear whether this was actually a manor house. It is therefore quite possible that these two views of the

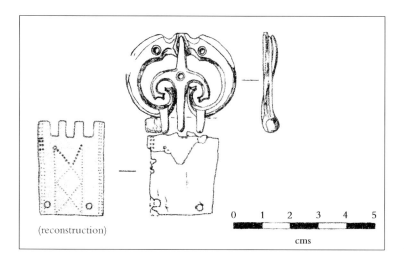

(reconstruction)

0   1   2   3   4   5

cms

**8** *The Stockwood Roman buckle.* Courtesy of Les Good

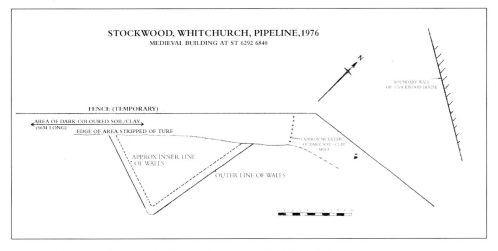

**9** *Plan of the medieval house at Stockwood.* Courtesy of M.W. Ponsford

origins of Bristol may not be mutually exclusive. If nothing else, at least it proves the continuity of urban planning in the Bristol area. One thing is certain however: its site on the banks of the Avon was of vital importance to its prosperity. Access to the Severn estuary gave it important trading links with Ireland, particularly Dublin and later the southern Irish towns, and important Midland cities such as Worcester and Chester. It also allowed Bristol to develop a profitable fishing industry by the next century. Barton Regis, the manor with which Bristol is paired in *Domesday Book*, stretched from what is now Barton Hill to Mangotsfield. Most of this was empty waste, such as the land now called St Philip's marsh, swampy even then. The inhabited, cultivated part was centred strongly on modern Barton Hill.

Bristol was a new town in an expanding urban landscape. The Romans had certainly settled the region earlier. Sea Mills, the Roman's *Abone*, was an important settlement and ferry station for troop movements up the Welsh coast. It was also the site of a villa, as were Brislington, Bedminster Down, Peter Street and Upper Maudlin Street in the area of St James Within in Bristol itself, Blaise Castle Hill, King's Weston, and Lawrence Weston in Henbury, Stafford Road in Baptist Mills, Watling Way in Shirehampton, Southmead and Filwood Park in Whitchurch. Other possible villa sites include Chessel Street in Bedminster, Clifton, Coombe Dingle, Horfield, St Bernard's Road in Shirehampton, and Westbury College and Bamfield at Whitchurch. Flax Bourton boasted a fortified township on what is now Gatcombe Farm.

Intriguingly, the late Roman finds from Bristol include a fourth-century Roman military buckle, discovered on land belonging to Hick's Gate Farm at Stockwood 0.62 miles (1km) from the villa complex at Keynsham. It has been suggested that the buckle belonged to a Germanic *foederatus* soldier, stationed at the town to protect it against incursions by barbarian raiders. It was similar Germanic *foederati*, including the Hengist and Horsa invited to

**10** *Entrance and north tower of Holy Trinity church, Westbury on Trym*

Britain by King Vortigern, who formed the earliest Anglo-Saxon presence in Britain, especially as there is evidence to suggest that the Anglo-Saxon estate of Keynsham was based very much on the earlier Roman villa, which was itself one of the settlements re-occupied in the later fourth century, possible by these same *foederati* mercenaries as payment for their services. Although this would seem to suggest that the Anglo-Saxon presence in this part of Bristol can be traced back to this early date, comparison with similar buckles found in burials at Gloucester suggests the alternative possibility that it belonged instead to a regular, non-Germanic Roman soldier. If nothing else, the presence of a military buckle of this date bears witness to the strong military presence in the area necessitated by the barbarian raiding and incursions faced by the late Roman Empire.

Despite these settlements, this part of the West Country remained relatively untouched by the Romans. *Abone*, the most important Roman settlement in the immediate Bristol region, although a populous and prosperous town, possessed relatively modest shops and buildings, without known hypocausts or bath sites and defences, and with only a few *tesserae* providing any evidence of the existence of mosaics. The most important Roman settlements were to the north and east: Gloucester (*Glevum*), Cirencester (*Corinium*) and Bath. Although a number of earlier Celtic sites were re-occupied, such as the hill forts of Maes Knoll and Stantonbury rings, and other sites, such as Frocester Court, Barnsley Park and Butcombe, and Stokeleigh, Bury Hill and Blaise Castle (where a group of graves were cut east to west in a temple site, itself enclosed within a hillfort), show a continuity of settlement from the Roman period, it was during the Saxon period that the region most markedly changed its character. Under the Romans, the pattern of nucleated villages settled within parishes did not exist. This is therefore a probable development of the Anglo-Saxons, assisted by the fusion of farms gradually running into each other. This process was given a filip after the conversion of the English, which brought with it the establishment of local parish churches around which the majority of villages developed. This process was only gradual however, and certainly not uniform. At Wharram Percy the scattered hamlets only merged into a consolidated village in the ninth or tenth centuries. Closer to home, the excavation of the abandoned village at Upton in Blockley showed that the siting of peasant longhouses around the village green only dates to the twelfth and thirteenth centuries. Many of the villages and settlements mentioned in the *Domesday Book* were still probably collections of scattered hamlets.

Bristol was surrounded by a number of Anglo-Saxon settlements which have now either been swallowed up in its urban sprawl, or become satellite towns. These include Westbury on Trym, Clifton, Bedminster, Redcliffe, Mangotsfield, Thornbury, Whitchurch, Keynsham, Pucklechurch, Oldland, Hanham, Hambrook, Harry Stoke, Aust, Bishopsworth, Brislington, Brentry, Stoke Bishop, Henbury, Bitton and Knowle. Mangotsfield, whose name records it was the field of one Mangoda, was already a satellite of Bristol by the time of the *Domesday Book*. Like Bristol it was part of the manor of Barton Regis, and Bristol church held three hides of land there. Redcliffe's position on the low hill overlooking the river and the names of its streets suggest that it, too, dates from the Saxon period. It may have been founded by the lords of Bedminster as a complement to Bristol on the opposite side of the Avon.

Somewhat later than the fourth-century Roman finds discovered at Stockwood were the remains of a medieval house and pottery found on top of a hill located just south of Stockwood House, south and west of Charlton Bottom. While the house itself dates only from the thirteenth century, some of the pottery is eleventh- and twelfth-century in date, indicating a long history of occupation at the site from at least those centuries.

Undoubtedly one of the wealthiest towns now in Bristol's orbit was Keynsham, then a royal manor, which the *Domesday Book* records as having belonged to Queen Edith, the wife of Edward the Confessor, whose posses-

**11** *Entrance to the north tower, home of Westbury church's Saxon grave slab*

sions in Somerset also included Milverton, Martock, Chewton Mendip, Batheaston and Bath. Keynsham had been the site of an Anglo-Saxon minster probably since the ninth century. The area under its jurisdiction was vast, about 13,000 acres (5,263ha) Attached to the *manerium* of Keynsham itself were the satellite settlements of Queen Charlton (derived from the Anglo-Saxon *Ceorlatun*, or *ceorl's* town), Chewton, Stanton Drew, Stanton Wick, Belluton, Burnett, and Pensford. The area now known as Pool Barton (derived from either *beretun*, corn farm, or *burhtun* fortified town/manor), which lies to the west of Keynsham parish church was probably the site of the original demesne land farmed by the landlord himself. As a royal manor, Keynsham naturally possessed a minster, which served as the mother church for the chapels at Charlton, Publow, Brislington and Whitchurch, then also known as Fylton, and situated somewhat further to the north-west than the modern village at Bamfield.

Whitchurch's status is unclear, as although it had definitely become attached to Keynsham by the fifteenth century, in 1065 Edward confirmed it as part of the property of the Bishop of Wells. Its name also presents a matter for some conjecture. Although it is traditionally considered to have its origins in a chapel dedicated to St White, the anchoress and patron of the Dorset church of Whitchurch Canonicorum, one of the minor *geneat* landowners in the Keynsham region was Wulfward White, whose surname may suggest that he had some part in the foundation of the church. White's wife, Edeva, possibly the Eddiva *Pulchra* (a translation of Eadgifu *Faira*, Eadgifu the Beautiful) of elsewhere in the *Domesday Book*, was a powerful woman in her own right, not only holding Burnett but also lands in Buckinghamshire in the 1060s. If she has indeed been correctly identified, then this formidable lady also held lands in Cambridgeshire, Essex, Hertfordshire, Lincolnshire, Suffolk and Yorkshire, possibly through her connection to the Godwin family. Another landlord

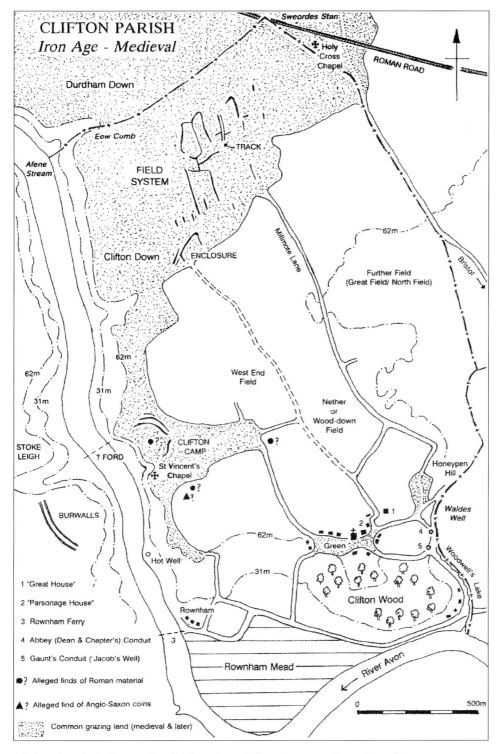

**CLIFTON PARISH**
*Iron Age – Medieval*

*Sweordes Stan*

Holy Cross Chapel

ROMAN ROAD

Durdham Down

*Eow Cumb*

TRACK

*Afene Stream*

FIELD SYSTEM

62m

Millmote Lane

Clifton Down    ENCLOSURE

Further Field (Great Field/ North Field)

Bristol

62m

62m

31m

31m

West End Field

Nether or Wood-down Field

STOKE LEIGH

? FORD

●?

CLIFTON CAMP

●?

St Vincent's Chapel

●?

▲?

Honeypen Hill

■ 1

Waldes Well

BURWALLS

62m

2

4

Green

5

Woodwell's Lake

Hot Well

31m

Clifton Wood

Rownham

1 "Great House"

2 "Parsonage House"

3 Rownham Ferry

4 Abbey (Dean & Chapter's) Conduit

3

5 Gaunt's Conduit ('Jacob's Well')

●? Alleged finds of Roman material

▲? Alleged find of Anglo-Saxon coins

Common grazing land (medieval & later)

Rownham Mead

River Avon

0                          500m

**12** *Iron Age, Anglo-Saxon and medieval remains at Clifton.* Courtesy of James Russell recorded in the 1060s was Wulfmer, who by the date of the compilation of the *Domesday Book* had been replaced by Aelfric of Keynsham, while Belluton was held by Sheriff Tovi of Somerset.

The Keynsham manor may have its origins in the seizure of the old Roman estates which were possibly based around the Roman house found at Somerdale, and belonged to the villa by the House of Cerdic in the first decades of the seventh century, perhaps to act as a buffer against the expanding power of Mercia. Excavations by Bristol Folk House Archaeological Society discovered the shaft of an Anglo-Saxon cross built into Keynshams abbey church's foundations, and also uncovered a grave slab cross, book clasp and a strap end, which would have covered the end of a Saxon man's belt. All these items dated from around the ninth and tenth centuries.

Bath was undoubtedly the most important ancient town in the region. It was, after all, the Roman spa town of *Aquae Sulis*, the Waters of the Goddess *Sul*. It was also an important administrative centre with an abbey, four churches, a mint, and (perhaps inevitably) three baths. Further south was the royal palace at Cheddar. Pottery finds in the area are rare before the tenth century, and only become common in the late eleventh and early twelfth. Thus much about the surrounding towns, and Bristol's relationship with them, remains unknown.

Several of the towns in the Bristol area had an important religious function. Westbury on Trym, for example (which then also covered much of what is now Redland and Stoke Bishop), had a minster church under royal patronage which held 50 hides (a hide was the measure of land considered sufficient to support a family) of the diocese of Worcester, far exceeding Bristol/Barton Regis, which only had six. This diocese covered much of what are now the counties of Worcestershire and Gloucestershire, excluding those parts which were on the western side of the Severn on the Welsh border. Apart from the minster itself, by the early twelfth century Westbury also possessed a chapel to St Werburgha, the daughter of King Wulfhere of Mercia, who was placed in charge of all the kingdom's female religious houses by her uncle Aethelred on his succession in 675. It was Aethelred who gave Bishop Oftor of Worcester 30 *cassates* of land at Henbury and Aust, and a fishery sometime around 691–2 and it is not impossible that her chapel dates from about this time, though there is no documentary evidence to support it.

Offa had inherited the land from his grandfather, Eanulf, who had been granted it by his cousin, King Aethelbald of Mercia, tax free for as long as the English remained Christian. With the king's permission, Eanulf founded a monastery at Bredon in 716-17, and another at Yate. The foundation of Westbury Church has been traditionally dated to these years, though again there is no evidence for this. At the minster, Westbury on Trym's monks were leading members of the tenth-century monastic revival. It had been founded by Offa of Mercia in 793-6 for the care of his soul ('*pro remedio animae meae*'), when he gave 60 hides at Westbury and ten *mansiones*/20 hides of land in Henbury to the church at Worcester in return for the customary services performed on the king's *feorm*. Its rents were two barrels of clear ale, seven cattle, six sheep, 40 cheeses, six measures of mead, 30 measures of rye and four measures of meal. In return for this, the peasants could pasture swine in the forest, from which they could gather firewood. They may even have been allowed to hunt small game.

In another charter of 794 Offa granted four *cassates* of land to his son Ethelmund. After the latter's death in battle in 804, his son Aethelric reasserted his rights to the property on his return from a pilgrimage at a synod convened at Clovesho. He then granted Westbury to his mother Ceolburga, abbess of Berkeley, though with the express prohibition of the abbey acquiring the land, and stipulating that it was to revert to the church at Worcester on her death. This did not occur, and 20 years later, in 824, the Mercian king Beornwulf was forced to call a second pontifical synod at *Clofesho* to decide the disputed ownership of the minster between the see of Worcester and Berkeley Abbey. The synod, presided over by Archbishop Wulfred and attended by ten bishops, nine *ealdormen*, a papal messenger, the king's brother and other nobles, ruled firmly in favour of Worcester.

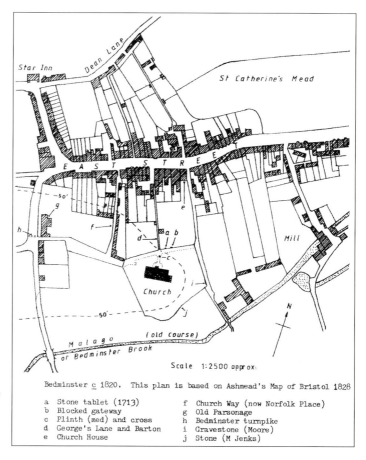

**13** *Bedminster, c. 1820, showing location of St John's church and Saxon village.*
Courtesy of
R.G.J. Williams

Bedminster c 1820. This plan is based on Ashmead's Map of Bristol 1828

| | | | |
|---|---|---|---|
| a | Stone tablet (1713) | f | Church Way (now Norfolk Place) |
| b | Blocked gateway | g | Old Parsonage |
| c | Plinth (med) and cross | h | Bedminster turnpike |
| d | George's Lane and Barton | i | Gravestone (Moore) |
| e | Church House | j | Stone (M Jenks) |

After Offa's death and the chaos of the Viking wars, much of the ecclesiastical land in Westbury was usurped by secular lords. This changed in 883 however when King Alfred appointed his son-in-law, the *ealdorman* Aethelred, to supervise the restoration of the alienated land back to the church. Aethelred duly returned the land back to its ecclesiastical lord, the abbot of Tewkesbury, who held it for the see of Worcester. The abbey was freed of all dues on its land, except for the royal *feorm*, in return for the surrender of 12 hides at Stoke Bishop and the payment of 30 *mancuses* of gold. The lay user, Cynulf, son of Geoluht, was still allowed to keep 12 hides of the land tax-free, though only on a three-generation lease from the church authorities and in return for the payment of 60 *mancuses* of gold.

Under St Dunstan's pupil, Oswald, who became bishop of Worcester in 960, Westbury became an integral part of the tenth-century monastic reform. Oswald wished to revitalise the English church by remodelling it after the continental monasticism of Cluny. As part of his programme Westbury, then a '*parochia* of his see', became the site of the first English Benedictine house, founded as a priory of St Mary *c*.963-4. Oswald appointed as prior of his new establishment Germanus of Fleury, who had come at Oswald's invitation to teach the Benedictine Rule, along with a priest and a number of novices. Although the parish system evolved long after the Anglo-Saxon period, the use of the term *parochia* here would seem to imply that the area already possessed a church, glebe land and the right to support itself from dues levied on the surrounding population. Their sojourn there was to be only temporary, however, as Oswald became concerned for their fate in the event of his death, and requested King Edgar to provide them with another site and endowment. In answer to his requests Aethelwine, the *ealdorman* of East Anglia, granted them a new site at Ramsey in the Huntingdonshire fens in 966, to which Oswald then once again transferred his flock. Possibly due to

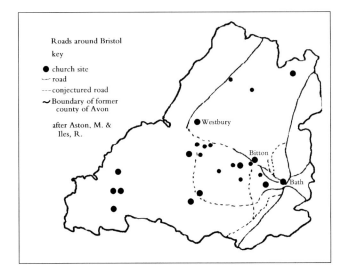

14 *Roman roads around Bristol.*
After M. Aston & R. Iles

friction between himself and the other monks, Germanus was transferred from Ramsey to Oswald's refounded house of Winchcombe, and the community was then headed by the former priest at Westbury, Agelnoth. In 969 Oswald then leased to his minister Aethelweard two *mansae* in Stoke Bishop, again for three generations. Fifteen years later in 984 Aethelweard, now described as Oswald's *miles*, 'soldier', perhaps indicating thegnly status, was granted an additional three *mansae* in Stoke Bishop, there called *Biscopes Stoce*, again on a three-generation lease for ten marks, with the property escheating to the bishopric of Worcester. By the time of the *Domesday Book* St Mary's of Worcester still held 50 hides of land in Westbury, which the Conqueror's clerks duly noted as including also the villages of Henbury, Redwick, Stoke Bishop and Yate.

The precise location of the boundary of Stoke Bishop has been a matter of considerable debate, but it seems probable that the Hazel *dene* mentioned in the 883 charter as forming part of the boundary is Ashley Brook, with the Hazel well associated with it a tributary spring, probably near the present Springfield Avenue. The next boundary mark, *Waldes Well*, 'Woodland Spring' in modern English, may have been what is now Mother Pugsley's Well; *Eowcumbe* could represent Walcombe Slade or its Gully running from the Downs to the Avon; *Hricgleage* is Ridge Lea; and *Pen Pau* is modern Pen Pole Wood, taking in also Clack Mill, the lead mines on Durdham Down before finally returning to Ashley Brook. The rivers Avon and Severn also formed part of the *tithing*'s boundaries, the first at Lamplighter's hall opposite Pill and the confluence of the Avon and the Trym, and the Severn on the path from Pen Pole Wood. Another interpretation may be that the Hazel *dene* mentioned in the charter in the valley of the Cran Brook, the *Waldes Well*, was one of a group of springs at the Clifton boundary on the former Woodwell Lane on what is now Jacob's Wells Road. *Sweordes Stan*, 'Sword's Stone' may refer to a point on the modern Stoke Road now marked by a group of late eighteenth- to early nineteenth-century mere stones. Ridge Lea, *Hricgleage*, may refer to Pen Pole Ridge, and the point on the Severn indicated by the charter may be at Elbury Gout. The *Lead Gedelf*, lead diggings mentioned in the charter, may be on the Downs, south-west of the round-about approaching the top of Parry's Lane. It could also be that the *Sweoperlna Stream*, 'the *Sweperl* Stream' of the 984 Stoke Bishop charter, was the Trym.

These landmarks describe the boundary between Stoke Bishop and Clifton which, like Barton Regis, contained 3 hides of land owned by Bristol Church. It had been held by Saewin, who had been Bristol's reeve under King Edward the Confessor. Unfortunately, the *Domesday* survey is the oldest documentary evidence for Clifton, and archaeological remains are similarly scant. The only artefacts recovered from the parish are coins of Aethelred, reputedly discovered in 1784 at Sion Row. It appears from the 883 charter that the Stoke estate consisted of two individual blocks of land corresponding to modern Stoke Bishop and Shirehampton, which, by the time of the *Domesday*

**15**  *The sole standing fragment of St Mary le Port church, now partly surrounded by the Bank of England*

*Book*, were separated by *Westone*, which formed the nucleus of the later Kings Weston and Laurence Weston.

Henbury, like Keynsham, may also have its origins in a Roman estate. The seventh-century grant of land to the Diocese of Worcester transfers it with its ancient boundaries, while similarities between the plan of Clifton parish and settlements in the Vale of Wrington – both laid out almost in strips – also suggest a similar continuity of settlement from Roman antiquity to the Middle Ages. Further north, the modern industrial suburb of Filton is recorded in the *Domesday Book* as part of Horfield, though its presence in history goes back to 770 when it was occupied by Abbot Tilhere of Berkeley, who was consecrated abbot of Worcester seven years later. Like Keynsham, Filton had a royal connection, with Goda, Edward the Confessor's sister, holding lands there.

Kington, a hamlet one mile west of Thornbury, was the site of the martyrdom of St Arild, one of the minor saints venerated by the English. Congresbury was revered as the resting place of St Congarus, a Welsh saint active in the conversion of the English in the sixth century, and whose feast day was 27 November. Bedminster, as its name suggests, was also an ecclesiastical settlement, probably centred on the now destroyed church of St John the Baptist, on the bluff on St John's Street overlooking the old course of the

Malago. This Saxon minster was the mother church of two other contemporary Bristolian foundations, the chapelries of St Mary Redcliffe, and Holy Trinity Church at Church Road, Abbots Leigh (which is recorded in the *Domesday Book* as held by Thurstan the Priest).

Other towns had distinct economic functions. Pucklechurch, where king Edmund was murdered on 26 May 946, was an important source of iron and possessed a market as well as a hunting lodge and a church. The *cweorn cleofu*, literally a quern (cleft?), mentioned in a charter at Pucklechurch may indicate that the town possessed a quarry for making quern stones. It is possible that this was located on the ridge south-east of Watley's End and east of the Frome, as the rock here is pennant sandstone suitable for making such hand-mills. It was still supplying iron in 1086, when the *Domesday Book* records there were six men who paid 90 lumps of iron. Stoke Bishop was a mining centre with a watermill. As well as the lead workings, Thornbury's origins are obscure, although it appears in documents around 896 under the spelling *Thornbyrig*. Its name meant 'the *bury* (town/settlement) where thorns grew' (according to the *Oxford Dictionary of English Place Names*). It was a parish and an important market, and, by virtue of this, like Bristol was at one time a borough. Also lying to the north of Bristol is Dyrham, a small settlement even then but known to the Anglo-Saxons as the site of the battle in 577 when the West Saxon kings Cuthwine and Ceawlin slew the British kings Coinmail, Condidan and Farinmail and won the 'three chesters' of Gloucester, Cirencester and Bath.

Also to the north of Bristol stretched the forest of Kingswood, *Kynggeswudu*, a vast hunting park 200 miles$^2$ (320km$^2$) in extent, covering an area from Little Avon in the north to the Bristol Avon in the south. At its western limit was the Severn estuary, while its eastern boundary was along what is now the A465 road. Although reserved for the pleasure of the king and nobles while hunting, it also provided the local people with an important source of wood for building and fuel, charcoal for the iron industry, and also fodder for pigs. The western most part of this forest was termed Fyllwood, a name connecting it to Fylton, suggesting that the villagers at Whitchurch had access to the wood's resources. By the time of the Norman Conquest about the same proportion of land had been cleared as around the time of the Second World War. By this estimate, only about 6-7.9 per cent of Gloucestershire and 4-5.9 per cent of Somerset was woodland.

Binding these settlements together was a network of roads and tracks allowing reasonably rapid communications between one settlement and another. Although most of these would have been simple tracks beaten into the ground by the constant passage of humans and animals, the old Roman roads were still very much in use. Bath in particular was well-served for roads, including part of the Roman Fosse Way. A road also ran from the town to Weston and North Stoke, probably passing through Bitton on its way over the River Boyd. Connecting Bath and Westbury on Trym was the old

Roman road leading to Sea Mills, possibly the *aeldna herepath*, the old military road of the 984 boundary charter of Stoke Bishop. From Westbury on Trym traffic could follow another Roman road from Sea Mills to Gloucester, an important route for trade and the rapid movement of troops. Most of Britain's modern roads follow the ancient routes of the Saxon period and before, and so communications in Anglo-Saxon England were probably very good. The only major parts of the Bristol region which were poorly served for roads were Kingswood in the north, and the south–western districts just beyond Bristol.

Despite this, the origins of these settlements are obscure, and this obscurity deepens in the case of Bristol. There is a dearth of contemporary written information about the place. The *Anglo-Saxon Chronicle* had only three entries concerning Bristol in the period of the Saxon kings, and all of these occurred during the reign of Edward the Confessor. It is mentioned as the departure point for Earl Godwine's sons Harold (the future King Harold who was to die at Hastings) and Leofwine to Ireland when Godwine fell from power in 1052. In 1062 Harold, then restored to the king's favour, used Bristol as a naval base to sail around Wales in the conflict against Gruffydd, prince of Gwynedd; and in 1067, after the Norman Conquest, Harold's dispossessed sons attacked Bristol by sea from Ireland, before being fought off. These incidents give an indication of Bristol's importance as a naval base and trading port, but lead us no nearer the mystery of its origins – a mystery which will be examined in the next chapter.

# 2  The origins of Bristol

No one really knows precisely when or why Bristol was founded. Despite its impressive strategic position, the royal charters granting the burgesses of Bristol certain privileges, which themselves attest to the growing prosperity and power of the town, only begin in the twelfth century. Nevertheless, the Anglo-Saxon kings were certainly not ignorant of the strategic importance of the Avon. The *Anglo-Saxon Chronicle* and the twelfth-century historian, Florence of Worcester, both mention Edward the Elder stationing parts of his army along the Severn from Cornwall to the mouth of the Avon, after a devastating raid earlier that year by the Viking jarls Ohtor and Hraold during which Cyfeiliog, bishop of Archenfield was captured. Despite being repulsed by the forces of Hereford, Gloucester and the surrounding cities, the two chieftains tried two more landings at Porlock and Watchet, before retreating to Ireland via Steepholme or Flatholme and Dyfed. Despite this obvious demonstration of the potential military importance of the site of the future Bristol, the *Chronicle* does not record its fortification, as it does for Warwick, Eddisbury, Chirbury, Runcorn and Buckingham, which were occupied and fortified by Edward around the date of the raid (*c*.914-16). Presumably even after this episode the existing borough forces, especially those of Hereford and Gloucester, were considered sufficient protection against such incursions, at least for another century.

Even *Domesday Book* only hints at Bristol's importance. The entry for Bristol is the smallest of any of the Gloucestershire towns, and is included in the entry for Barton Regis, a *cynges tun* or royal manor. The *Domesday Book* merely states that the manor had a population of 74, comprising 22 villagers, 25 smallholders, 18 freedmen and nine slaves. This, however, should not be taken as a true estimate of the town's population, as estimates of the size of any pre-Conquest English borough based on *Domesday* statistics will be too low. It does not mention the town's size or population, nor any trade or industries carried on in the town, merely stating that Bristol and Barton Regis pay the king 110 marks of silver, and Geoffrey of Coutances 33 marks of silver and one mark of gold. The entry does hint however that the town was bigger than the manor. Barton Regis is described as *Bertune apud Bristou*, Barton quite close to Bristol, which suggests that Bristol was better known and more important than the manor with which it is listed. But suggest is all it does; and there are no other facts about the city.

Bristol, however, is not alone in this. Although 71 boroughs are mentioned in the *Domesday Book*, there are a number of glaring omissions. It does not include the two most important towns in eleventh-century England, London and Winchester, and is similarly neglectful of Tamworth, Hastings, Hythe and Romney. Apart from these places, there were other sections of the population left out. The *Domesday* survey did not count women, except in rare cases, and knights and clergy tended to be omitted. The survey is also silent about the number of children these people had. This is not surprising, as the *Domesday* survey was primarily economic in nature. It was not felt that the clergy, aristocracy or children were active in the creation of wealth, and, except in a few cases where a group of widows held a ploughteam between them, women's activity was confined largely to their private household. *Domesday Book* is concerned almost solely with landholding, and so would not count the wives of serfs as serfs could not hold land, and, unlike their husbands, it seems assumed that women never worked on the land. Similarly, the bulk of the urban population seems to be excluded for the same reason. The *Domesday Book* reflects the concerns of a feudal society, which measured wealth and power in terms of land. The urban population of craftsmen and merchants were outside the formal landholding structure of feudal society, and so the mass of them simply were not counted either.

Despite these difficulties, the total population of Bristol in the late eleventh century has been estimated at around 1,000-2,000 people. This estimate may well be too conservative, however. Recent excavations of Viking York forced historians and archaeologists to revise their views of the size of the population, as they showed that the town was far more populous than expected. Bristol also had a large itinerant population. Drovers came to Bristol from Wales, merchants from Ireland and other traders presumably from Bristol's economic hinterlands in the West Country. Even if this estimate is small, it nevertheless compares well with Gloucester's population of *c*.3,000, and London's of 12,000. The total population of Gloucestershire and Bristol was about 35,000-36,000 in 1086, with an average population density of about five to ten people per square mile (1.3km²). If nothing else, it shows that by the time of the Viking wars English society was returning to a level of urbanisation previously known only under the Romans. Most Roman towns had a population of about 2,000-3,000 people. Although Bristol had not quite reached that level of population, it does bear witness to the revival of town life in Anglo-Saxon England and the dynamism of a growing urban economy.

Despite its shortcomings, the survey does indicate the town's growing strength by the amount of tax it paid. Those 110 marks paid to the king are Bristol's 'farm of one night' (*firma unius noctis* or '*feorm*' in Anglo-Saxon), as were the rents levied by Offa on his estate at Westbury on Trym: the amount of provisions required to support the royal household for one day. Although, like those of Westbury, most of the payments were in kind, and many remained so until the time of Henry II; during the reign of Edward the Confessor these payments were being increasingly rendered in cash. The expense involved in entertaining the king and his retinue was heavy.

Sometimes it required a group of estates to provide enough for a day's *firma*, which already by the time of Edward could be as much as £80. Of the revenue gained from the boroughs, the king shared a third with the local earl, presumably for his aid in organizing its defence and maintenance. This may be why £33 of its revenue went to its new Norman lord, Geoffrey of Coutances, in the *Domesday Book*. Bristol's, Barton Regis' and Mangotsfield's combined *feorm* of 110 marks separate them as one of England's more prosperous manors. However many of them there were, the people of Bristol were obviously becoming very wealthy.

This pairing of Barton Regis and Bristol has led some historians to compare Bristol with other pairs of palaces and *burhs* (such as Cheddar and Axbridge), and to conclude that Bristol was founded as a port and market to serve the already existing royal estate of Barton Regis. It was certainly the case that during the tenth century a number of royal manors became increasingly important nationally through the settlement of traders attracted by the better conditions in the neighbourhood of royal residences. By the time of 1066, this pairing seems to have been sufficiently widespread for a number of royal manors to count *burgenses* as well as *villani* among their population. It may well have been market forces which encouraged the setting up of the mint. Communities of merchants and the financial demands of their royal overlord made them centres for the passage and exchange of money, which created the demand for a mint. By the time of the Norman Conquest, however, trade had caused Bristol to flourish to such an extent that it outgrew the relationship with Barton Regis. Geoffrey of Coutances therefore built the castle as a new point of control for this mercantile centre.

Another, older view is that Bristol was a Viking settlement, founded to trade with the Norse colonies in Ireland. Although Bristol lies far outside the Danelaw (the area occupied by the Vikings during their invasion of England), Viking artefacts have been found in Bristol, and the Norsemen did found towns on the other side of the estuary, such as Swansea. There is a strong link between the eleventh-century pottery of Bristol and Dublin, and Bristol was notorious for exporting English slaves overseas to Ireland.

This link between the West Country and Viking Ireland pre-dates Bristol, with economic bonds between the two regions going back to the Bronze Age. These connections were strengthened between 980-1000, when Chester lost its monopoly on Irish trade to the great market towns of the Bristol Channel; and signs of this can be seen in the Irish coinage of the period. Some of the earliest Dublin coins seem to take those of West Country mints as their models, including those of Bath and Watchet in Somerset, and Totnes and Lydford in Devon. It was not just the designs which crossed the Irish Sea; a Gloucester coin was found amongst a hoard buried at Kildare in 991, and another coin from Bath was found at Dungarvan, having been hidden somewhat later. This implies these coins were exported to Ireland through Bristol, and provides firm evidence that trade with Ireland was increasing. It would be a mistake to put too much stress on this, however. Bristol's economic activities were probably growing on a number of fronts, and Ireland was only one part of an expanding network of internal trade. The estuary provided the opportunity for trade down the coast to Cornwall, across to Wales and up to Gloucester and beyond.

It is coinage which in fact provides an important clue as to precisely when Bristol came into existence. It seems that minting first began in Bristol during the last years of Aethelred II, with coins of the last small cross type. These were cast by Aelfweard, a moneyer, who may have been the same Aelfweard active at the Worcester and Wallingford mints. During the reign of Cnut, five moneyers, Aegelwine, Aelfwine, Godaman, Wulfwine and Wynsige, were employed at the mint, and it is from this period that the numismatic evidence for Bristol's existence is clearest. Minting was one of the major activities of Bristol, and the mint continued, with interruptions, for nearly 700 years before it was closed in 1698 during the reign of William of Orange.

One last theory of Bristol's origins needs to be mentioned: that it was founded as an ecclesiastical centre. The principal evidence for this is the Harrowing of Hell relief now in Bristol Cathedral. This originally formed part of a carved frieze, although when it was found in 1832 it had been used as a grave cover. It was discovered during digging at College Green in a small late Saxon cemetery associated with the church of St Augustine the Less. These burials were discovered during archaeological investigation of the site after it had suffered bomb damage during the War. Its proximity to the abbey of St Augustine, now Bristol Cathedral, has led Professor Dickenson to speculate that the abbey was founded sometime during the Dark Ages, and preserves a tradition of St Augustine of Canterbury having visited the area in 603.

The antiquarian John Leland recorded in his itinerary in the 1540s a tradition then current among Bristolians that the site had been visited by St Augustine of Canterbury when he met the leaders of the Celtic church that year at Aust. The site of the modern abbey was, asserted Leland, the final resting place of St Jordan, one of the monks accompanying St Augustine. Bede in his *Ecclesiastical History* recorded that there was indeed a meeting between St Augustine and representatives of the Celtic church in 603, at a place still known in his time as St Augustine's Oak, to urge the Celtic Christians to adopt Catholic practices, especially over the calculation of the date of Easter. He does not, however, mention any monk called Jordan, and notes only that St Augustine's Oak was on the border between the Hwiccas and West Saxons. This description could apply to any place on the southern Gloucestershire border, extending not just along the boundary with Somerset but also with Wiltshire.

Aust first appears in 691 as *Austin* and in 794 as *Austan*, possibly a form of the name *Augustus* or *Augustinus*. It could simply be a reference to the Roman Second Legion, the *Legio Augusta*, who crossed the Severn in the second century. Roman finds from the construction of the Severn Bridge and linguistic evidence that the Aust Passage (*Trajectus Augusti* from its connection with Caerleon on Usk, and given the name *Iscia Legio Augusta* after its role as the seat of the Augustan Legion) was so called during the Roman period, would seem to support an identification of Aust with the *Augustinus* at which Bede records St Augustine meeting the British bishops. In Bristol the association with St Augustine also seems to be quite ancient. There was certainly a chapel dedicated to St Jordan on College Green in the later Middle Ages, and the abbey was always referred to as 'St Augustine's, Bristol' in official documents. This is very unusual: Augustinian houses generally were referred to by the name of the place in which they were situated, such as Keynsham, for example. The stress on the name of the house's patron saint seems to suggest that there was indeed a quite ancient association between the place and St Augustine when Robert Fitzharding chose to site his monastery on the spot in the twelfth century.

Furthermore, while the Latin term *locus* and Old English *stow* usually mean simply 'place', quite often the term implies a place of religious assembly. The lack of evidence for Bristol as an early centre of secular administration, coupled with the evidence of the Harrowing of Hell relief and burials from St Augustine the Less, dated to the Saxo-Norman period, suggest that not only was St Augustine's cult already present in the City, but that it was also responsible for part of the City's name, if nothing else. There are few dedications to St Augustine of Hippo during this period (one being a joint dedication to him and St Olaf at Wellow Abbey near Grimsby), and it seems likely that there must have already been a tradition connecting the saint and the site of his later abbey to warrant its foundation in the twelfth century.

The oldest church in Bristol, however, was St Peter's, founded to serve Barton Regis. Anglo-Saxon finds at Tower Lane and Redcliffe, as well as the relief at Bristol Cathedral, indicate that the city also had its origins in a number of small, separate settlements associated with particular parish churches. These small villages gradually became absorbed by the new *burh* at Barton Regis as it prospered and expanded, just as it was poised to do to Clifton, Redland and Redcliffe by the end of the eleventh century.

# 3  Law and defence

Although surprising to modern eyes, government and the military were inseparable in the Middle Ages. The local lords were responsible for justice on their estates, and also organised police and military operations to catch criminals and fight invaders, such as the Vikings or raiders from Wales. When Alfred and Athelstan set up the *burhs*, they saw them as forming part of a trading and defensive network around England. Indeed many of them (particularly the smaller *burhs* such as Halwell and Pilton, which seem never to have been built for trade or habitation), are forts in all but name. Those *burhs* which also acted as market centres were called ports, a term borrowed from the France of Charlemagne. A port could be any place where commerce took place, regardless of its location – it might be far inland, away from the sea. Supervising its administration on behalf of the port's lord was the portreeve. The portreeve was the urban equivalent of the sheriff, or shire-reeve, who oversaw the administration of the rural shires. He collected the tolls and rents, and witnessed the commercial transactions within the town. Just as the shires had their courts, so did the *burhs*. The borough courts by the laws of King Edward had to meet three times a year to hear criminal cases and discuss the administration of the port. In addition to this, the *burhs* also held a number of hides of the surrounding land, which were responsible for their maintenance. Bristol was also responsible for a couple of hundreds. The hundred was the smallest Anglo-Saxon administrative district. It was so called because it was originally conceived as a unit of 100 hides of land, the hide being the unit of land sufficient to support a family. As time progressed, the size of the hundred changed according to local custom: not all hundreds now included 100 hides of land. The hundred court met in the open air every four weeks under the supervision of the king's reeve. Each hundred had a royal villa at its centre, and a similar system prevailed in Wales. This suggests that the system may have been based on Roman administrative practices, which were taken over or copied by the Saxons.

There is some confusion about borough courts; few documents refer to them, and often the descriptions are ambiguous. It is unclear, for example, whether the borough court mentioned in a certain document is a body solely concerned with justice in that town, or whether it is a shire or a hundred court which just happens to meet in that particular borough. It does seem though that when Edgar ordered the *buruhgemot* (town council/court) to meet three times a year, he was actually referring to courts which specifically administered boroughs, as distinct from shires or hundreds. Some boroughs in southwestern England, such as Bedwyn and Warminster, seem to have been too small to have warranted a borough court. These two were like Bristol in that they were attached to a royal manor, and so it seems that in these instances the king would also act to protect his rights over the citizens by ruling them directly, not through a special court. It may be that Bristol, too, could have been considered too small to warrant a borough court.

Bristol's situation within the jurisdictional areas is also confused and unclear. In the *Domesday Book* Bristol is included in the Somerset hundred of Hartcliffe with Bedminster, which apart from these places also included its modern suburb of Knowle. It also appears in the Gloucestershire hundred of Swinehead, along with its parent manor of Barton Regis, Clifton, Hanham, Mangotsfield, Bitton, Hambrook, Oldland, Harry Stoke and Winterbourne. Aust, Henbury, Redland, Westbury on Trym and Stoke Bishop were in the separate hundred of Brentry, with Stoke Bishop a *tithing*, a further administrative subdivision, of Westbury on Trym. Bristol's apparent incorporation into the hundreds of Swinehead and Hartcliffe could be due to jurisdiction over Bristol being divided between Somerset and Gloucestershire. The division of a village between two different manors was not uncommon. Iron Acton, for example, had been split between the lords Ebbi and Harold (not Harold Godwinson, the king). It could also reflect men of different lords living in the same town, as could happen under feudalism. The rectilinear pattern of the *burhs* suggest that the standard practice was to let out the land in blocks, representing small estates to individual landlords, who would then subdivide it into small plots which would be held by the eventual occupiers as the town became more successful. This method of development meant that the tenements grew in long, narrow strips, though each retained a valuable bit of street front. It also meant the urban population could be under a number of different landlords. Even when the borough was on the royal demesne, the king frequently alienated tenements, customs and jurisdiction to another landlord. Aethelred and Aethelflaeda of Mercia granted the bishop of Worcester half their rights over the city 'in market-place or in street' in return for spiritual services after they fortified the town at his request. The £33 which went to Geoffrey of Coutances aside from Bristol's *feorm* could be the result of William having alienated some of the royal rights in his favour after Geoffrey built the Castle, following Aethelred's and Aethelflaeda's precedent. Landlords were also keen to acquire property in towns. By the time of the *Domesday Book*, Leicester had 134 houses, which were attached to 27 different manors.

The confusion over the hundred in which Bristol lay may be due to a similar process of subinfeudation. Aelfgar, lord of Bishopsworth, for example, held 10 houses in Bristol. The manor of Brentry owned two houses in the city at the time of the *Domesday Book*, and three hides either in the town or Barton Regis belonged to St Mary's of Worcester. It may also indicate that there was a borough court, *buruhgemot*, in Bristol, which had jurisdiction over those two hundreds of Swinehead and Hartcliffe with Bedminster, or simply that both hundreds happened to hold their courts in the city. Although it cannot be ruled out that Bristol was not blessed with a borough court, it would be surprising if that were the case, considering the town's population made it one of the 20 largest towns in England. It does seem that Bristol possessed some local autonomy, which was lost immediately after the Conquest. Although later charters granted Bristolians certain trading rights, they still had to plead their cases before the shire court in Gloucester. A considerable amount of power was restored to them in 1188, however, when Henry II exempted Bristolians from the jurisdiction of all courts other than their own borough courts and those courts conducting royal business.

Barton Regis hundred, however, including modern Barton Hill, Clifton, Downend, Stapleton and Blackswarth, retained its court until *c.*1800, when it was abolished. Although its correct title of Court Leet and View of Frankpledge was a twelfth-century innovation, in its structure it remained remarkably true to its Anglo-Saxon ancestry. *Leet* is an old term for a manor court, and both the term and vestiges of its original function remain in Taunton and Watchet court leets, held annually. The term *frankpledge* meant 'peace pledge', and attests to the court's origins as an institution for enforcing the king's peace on his land. Its 'view' was the inquiry into the state of the *tithings* held for a few days every year by the sheriff at the hundred courts, attendance at which was compulsory for every free man. These *tithings*, each under the jurisdiction of a *tithingman*, were the ten lesser areas into which every hundred was further divided. Bristol during the 1040s lay in the sprawling earldom of Swein, which included much of Gloucestershire and Somerset. After the disgrace of the Godwin family in 1051, the south-western shires of Devon, Cornwall, Dorset and Somerset were given to Earl Odda. After their restoration in 1052, Bristol passed into the hands of Harold, the future king who would fall at Hastings, his brother having died in exile in Constantinople. Harold's new earldom covered the whole of the former kingdom of Wessex, with the exception of Kent and East Anglia, which were given to Leofric and Gyrth.

As for the towns' defences, these followed a common pattern. Most *burhs* were surrounded by a rampart made of clay, or clay and turf, reinforced with wood. The ramparts sloped at the back towards the town, for easy access by the defenders, but were vertical or very steep at the front to make storming them as difficult as possible. They were usually 2-3m high and 9-12m wide, and it is thought that they were crowned by a wooden palisade as an additional defence. In a number of cases these ramparts were strengthened by additional material and the replacement of the wooden palisade by a stone wall. Inside these outer ramparts many *burhs* had a system of defensive ditches based on Roman military ideas.

Unfortunately, no obvious remains of the Saxon defences have yet been found. Professor Rahtz's excavations of St Mary le Port Street led him to suggest that part of the original defensive ditch lay under Dolphin Street. This is now impossible to corroborate as Dolphin Street has now been overlaid with the Wine Street Car Park; and Rahtz himself has now rejected the idea. This really is not surprising, as the Saxon town lies in the busiest heart of Bristol, a site that has been redeveloped and built over time and again. Many *burh* fortifications were destroyed in the eleventh century, probably by Cnut around 1016. As a Viking king, Cnut would obviously not be well-disposed to towns fortified against him and his countrymen. Lydford and South Cadbury were among those *burhs* whose defences were destroyed. The ramparts were pulled down, and the ditches filled in – yet enough of the fortifications remain to be readily identifiable. Bristol's street plan is, however, highly suggestive of the course of the original Saxon walls, and despite Prof. Rahtz's rejection, the St Mary le Port ditch still remains a plausible possibility for the earliest east end of the Saxon enclosure. Elsewhere, the course of the town walls are suggested by the remains of the twelfth-century Norman wall, such as the possible bank discovered on the west side of Small Street, tentatively dated to the eleventh to twelfth centuries, which may have been a precursor to the later Norman walls. It is also possible that the earthen defences and east gate of Geoffrey of Coutance's castle were originally part of the late Saxon *burh* itself, taken over and incorporated by the Norman engineers into their new fortification. Like their Saxon precursor, however, the precise position of many portions of the Norman wall are obscure, and although the evidence is suggestive, it has not been conclusively proven that there actually was such a rampart upstream of the Bridge towards the Castle.

# 4 Buildings and architecture

No overview of any city would be complete without saying something about the city's hard shell: its buildings. Unfortunately, so much of Anglo-Saxon Bristol has been built over during successive centuries, and so much was unrecorded by contemporaries, that much of the city's layout and appearance remains unknown. However, the excavations of Tower Lane, Castle Park and St Mary le Port Street, and comparison with similar sites elsewhere, give us tantalizing clues.

To the Anglo-Saxons the most important building in a town or village would have been its church. Religion was at the centre of medieval life, informing their concepts of law and justice, and even government itself. The church building itself was a focus of community life. Within its walls people saw and heard the sacred drama of the liturgy, as well as engaging in secular activities such as industry: in the earliest remains at St Mary le Port church, there are indications of two hearths and an area of burnt soil suggesting that the church was being used as a workshop, aside from its religious dedication.

Anglo-Saxon England boasted about 2,600 known parish churches, of which about 500 still survive in some form or other. Most of these date from the great explosion of church building in the late tenth to early eleventh century, around the year 1000. The majority of these churches were established by local landlords to serve their estates, although urban churches were far from unknown. The beginnings in the eleventh century of urbanisation, which would flourish so spectacularly in the twelfth, led to 30 churches in London, and 24 in Norwich, for example. The density of the churches within the core site of the Saxon *burh* in Bristol is typical of pre-Conquest towns.

In Bristol, unfortunately, no church from this period seems to have survived. St Mary le Port, St Ewen, Christ Church and All Saints may well have been Anglo-Saxon foundations, but there is no clear evidence to support this, although the lower part of the west tower of St Peter's is probably eleventh-century, testifying to the church's Saxon origins. Within the precincts of the later castle, the chapel of St Martin, the south wall of which has been excavated and which stood in the Castle's outer ward facing what is now Castle Green to the north, may also have originally been a late Saxon church retained by the Normans for the Castle when the rest of the site was levelled. At Earl's Barton in Northamptonshire, a late Saxon church has survived within an extensive earthwork, which may thus also be Anglo-Saxon. If the Norman castle at Bristol did partially incorporate the defences

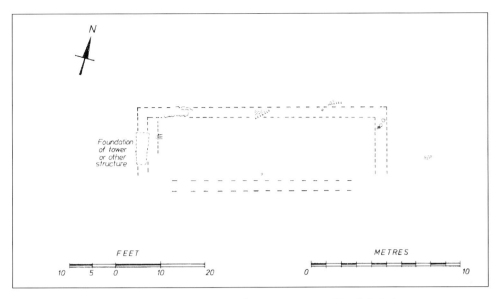

**16** *Conjectured plan of the Saxon church, St Mary le Port.* Courtesy of Prof. P. Rahtz

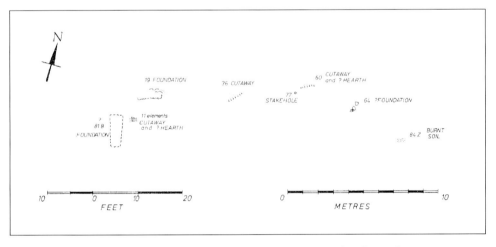

**17** *Archaeological remains of the Saxon levels, St Mary le Port.* Courtesy of Prof. P. Rahtz

of the Saxon *burh*, then it is possible that, as at Earl's Barton, the church within those defences may similarly have survived, or at least been superseded by a Norman church founded on the same spot. Excavations at St Mary le Port indicated that there was a building on the site in this period, measuring approximately 14-15m in length and 4m in width, with a foundation at the west end to support a tower. No more can be said about this, and it has been said that even this is little more than guesswork.

What the exterior of the church looked like is similarly unknown. It could have been built of stone, or wood, or both. The Anglo-Saxons preferred

**18** *Harrowing of Hell relief, Bristol Cathedral*

wood as a building material, but stone was certainly used as well. The roofs of most churches were probably thatched, but small triangular shingles of wood were also used, and a few important churches used lead sheets. At Monkwearmouth the church roof followed Roman practice and was built of thin limestone slates and lead flashings. Towers were a late Saxon innovation in church architecture, and may well have been inspired by the *campanili* on Italian churches. In most places the church was constructed of materials that were available locally. As has been noted, there are indications of quarrying around Bristol. The foundations of the first church on the site of St Mary le Port were of Brandon Hill Grit and Pennant Sandstone, while at the north and east areas of this church were the possible remains of Pennant Sandstone walls. It may very well be that the church was built either wholly or partly of stone. Traces of buff-coloured mortar were found on stones from this period, which were incorporated into the later churches, which suggests that the exterior was similarly of buff-mortared stone. At the west end of the church, however, was a line of timber posts indicating that part of the church's structure, at least, was wooden.

As to what the interior looked like, little can be said except that there was no aisle. It is also quite likely that the walls of the church were richly decorated with carvings and paintings depicting scenes from the Bible. Sculptures of angels and Christ may have been fairly common, as a number have survived quite apart from the *Harrowing of Hell*, relief now in Bristol Cathedral. The walls of medieval churches were covered in murals; and examples still survive from the Anglo-Saxon period. A fragment from the New Minster at Winchester, possibly depicting a heavenly choir, has been preserved, while the paintings of angels from the nave of the church at Nether Wallop in Hampshire are also excellent examples of the Saxon painter's art.

These murals would have been painted on the plaster covering the churches' stonework, not on the bare stones themselves. The exterior of the church was also plastered, and whitewash and coloured plaster may have been used as well. At Bibury in Gloucestershire the drilled lathe supports for the plaster can be still be seen, while pinkish plaster covered the church at Monkwearmouth. Stucco, a mixture of plaster and paint, was also used, for example on the crossed capitals at Milburne Port, and to cover the carving of the Virgin Mary at Deerhurst, again in Gloucestershire.

No discussion of Anglo-Saxon church carving and painting would be complete without mentioning the *Harrowing of Hell* relief in Bristol Cathedral. This shows Christ rescuing figures from hell, and is taken from the Biblical and apocryphal story of Christ's descent into hell to raise up the sinners after He died on the cross. This subject was becoming very popular in Anglo-Saxon art in the eleventh century, though it had been depicted both in England and on the Continent sometime before: the oldest extant wall painting of it dates from 705-7 in Santa Maria Antiqua in Rome, where Christ is shown treading on a swarthy, bound Satan and raising up two clothed figures. Byzantine artists

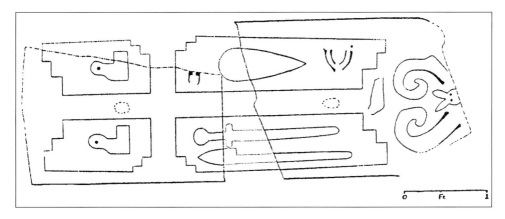

**19** *Saxon grave slab, All Saints, Westbury on Trym.* Drawing by Edwin George

45

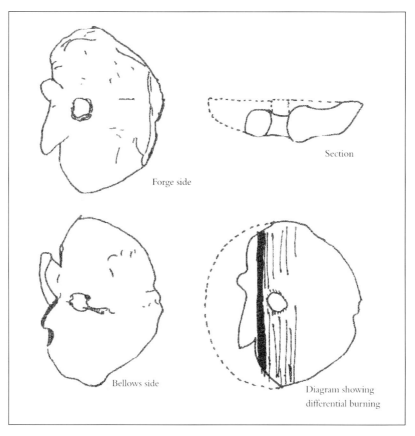

Forge side

Section

Bellows side

Diagram showing
differential burning

**20** *Forge stone from Bristol Castle.* After Ponsford

called the subject *anastasis*, or 'raising up', and a Byzantine mural contemporary with Bristol's *Harrowing of Hell* exists in Daphne.

Although the descent of Christ into hell is mentioned in the New
Testament, the immediate influence on its depiction was the apocryphal
Gospel of Nicodemus in which Christ 'plucked Adam out of Hell by the right
hand; and all the saints followed after them' (according to Michael Swanton's
translation for Penguin). This in turn inspired native Anglo-Saxon literary
treatments of the same theme, such as the poem 'Christ and Satan'. The image
of Christ trampling on beasts had its origins in Psalm 91, verse 13: 'You will
tread upon the lion and the cobra, you will trample the great lion and the
serpent'. This found pictorial expression in Roman depictions of the Emperor
Constantine holding a cross staff and treading on a dragon. The depiction of
Christ holding out his hand to rescue the sinners has a similar later Roman
origin in coins showing the Emperor extending his hand to liberate the
citizens of conquered territories.

One of the most influential sources for the introduction of the image of the
*Harrowing of Hell* was the *Utrecht Psalter*, produced in the second quarter of the
ninth century at Hautvilliers near Rheims, and brought to England around

AD 1000. No fewer than three copies were made in the Canterbury scriptorium, the earliest dated soon after its arrival in the early eleventh century. The *Utrecht Psalter* shows hell as the head of a giant or monster, as well as a human head spitting fire, an image which also appears in a late eighth- or early ninth-century English ivory carving of the Last Judgment. Other artifacts which no doubt played a role in the development and spread of the iconography of Christ's *Harrowing of Hell* include the ivory book-covers from Genoels-Elderen in Belgium, the German diptych now in the Kaiser Friedrich-Museum in Berlin, and a reliquary (now in the Victoria and Albert Museum) showing Christ bearing a cross staff and rescuing sinners from the jaws of hell. Other close parallels include the Copenhagen and Hereford Gospels. The depiction of hell as a dragon-like beast, or even as a dog, may be ultimately derived from early Christian images of Jonah in the whale, and the Old Testament monster Leviathan; both the *Utrecht Psalter* and the *Caedmon* manuscript, produced *c*.AD 1000 in Canterbury, show hell as the mouth of a dog or dragon in profile.

Nearer home, the subject appears in stone carvings at the south end of the churches at South Cerney and Quenington. Although these may be Norman, they are certainly still part of the Anglo-Saxon artistic tradition. The carving itself is part of the Winchester school of art, and shows marked similarity to contemporary manuscript illustrations of the subject, such as the *Quinity* miniature, of *c*.1023-35, the New Minster *Liber Vitae*, of *c*.1031, and most notably *Cotton Tiberius C.vi*, the *Tiberius Psalter*, dated to some time after 1066. Like the Bristol relief this shows hell as a beast, though it also peculiarly shows Satan's legs bound at the back. Its strong similarities to the *Tiberius Psalter* suggest that the Bristol relief was also carved some time in the 1060s. It was probably part of a frieze, but its trapezoidal shape might suggest that it stood alone, as does a similar-shaped carving of the Madonna and Child at Beverstone Church near Tetbury. On the other hand, it could have formed part of the composition of a rood screen, as did the pair of angels in flight at the church of Bradford on Avon, and may be observed on screens at Breamore and Headboure Worthy, Hampshire. The Bristol relief is comparable to these, and similar in size to the relief set in the south tower of Beverstone Church of the Ascension, which shows similar artistic parallels (in the bent knees of Christ and flowing draperies) to the Bradford on Avon relief. Other aspects of the relief's execution, such as the roped hair, hunched left shoulder, Christ's distinctive stance, its trapezoidal shape, and the sculptural technique of scooping out the unwanted stone, are all shared by other examples of pre-Conquest sculpture.

The stone from which the relief was carved is Jurassic Limestone, though not from the local sources at Dundry or Doulting. This probably indicates that figural sculptors were not itinerants, wandering from place to place as their work led them, but operated near the best source of their stone and worked from patterns from the ecclesiastical centre. This system certainly existed on the Continent: in France, capitals and sarcophagi were made in the foothills of the Pyrenees, and exported far to the north to the valleys of the Seine and Rhône.

It is to continental examples again that we must look to get an idea of what the relief may have looked like originally, since the surface of the stone has been worn away through the centuries. The mural of the *Descent into Hell* at Muestair in Switzerland, dating from the ninth century, may be especially useful. This relief shows Christ in a coloured gown with dark bands and white sleeves. Christ's face and hands, and the bodies of the sinners in hell, are coloured naturalistically, and the mouth, eyes, hair and nails are all carefully detailed and picked out. If the Bristol relief was similarly coloured, its effect would have been just as impressive.

Our relief presents a problem chronologically and stylistically. It is more than a century older than the church in which it was found, and predates the surviving portions of all of Bristol's churches. On the other hand, its discovery in the nineteenth century, when the eighteenth-century floor was taken up and the Chapter House returned to the level of the twelfth-century floor, suggests that it was found above rather than below these levels. Furthermore, the subject of the *Harrowing of Hell* remained popular in the twelfth century, other examples surviving from Lincoln Cathedral, and Shobdon, Eardisley and Billesley in Herefordshire. Shobdon was the first Victorine Augustinian community in Britain, and the predecessor to Bristol. The solid execution of the Bristolian figure of Christ, whose draperies have been viewed as being more in the tradition of Romanesque linearity than Winchester fluidity, along with the prevalence of similarly roped hair in Romanesque sculpture, could also suggest that the Bristol relief was the predecessor of the later twelfth-century monuments. Its size makes it probable that it was actually produced within the City, rather than transported. It may be the sole surviving remnant of the chapel of St Jordan, the site of which is now occupied by the cathedral. From the surviving roods still remaining in their original place, it seems likely that it was placed over a doorway to mark the main entrance to the church. Although it remains unknown whether it did indeed form part of a frieze, the existence of other similar reliefs in the region suggests the existence of local workshops producing other sculptural works on a similarly large scale. On the other hand, the piece's rough execution, smooth, untreated surfaces and lack of architectural framework may suggest that it was discarded, as for one reason or another it was never finished. One thing is certain despite these questions: in this relief Bristol possesses a glorious masterpiece of Anglo-Saxon art.

Another fascinating survival of Anglo-Saxon carving in Bristol is the grave slab now incorporated into the ceiling of the stairwell of the north tower of Holy Trinity Church, Westbury on Trym. The grave slab, now divided into two, shows a cross surrounded by a number of other emblems, tentatively identified as a horseshoe, kite shield, axe, sword and the possible matrices of brass plates, now vanished, showing two small kneeling figures, each also with an inscription at their foot, also lost. At the bottom of the slab are the remains of scrollwork. It is believed that the slab dates from the eighth century and originally bore only the cross and scroll. Subsequently, the kite shield, sword, axe and horseshoe were added sometime around 1100 when the slab was appropriated for the tomb of a Saxon *thegn* or Norman knight, probably the latter as, unlike the Norman knights, the Anglo-Saxons fought on foot and so would have felt little need to have themselves commemorated with the trappings of horsemanship suggested by horseshoes. Then, in the early fifteenth century, the two brasses were added as the grave slab was yet again appropriated for use for another member of the local nobility, before being finally incorporated into the tower as humble building material during Bishop Carpenter's reconstruction of the church in 1447. The slab's long career not only shows the antiquity of settlement in Westbury on Trym, but also its

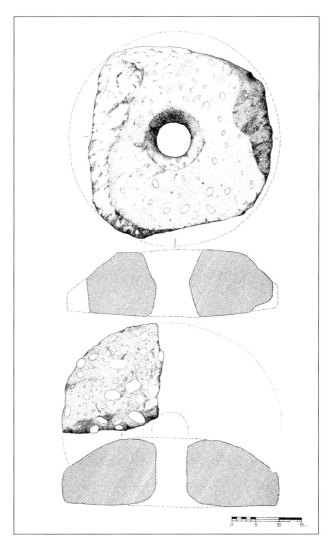

**21** *Saxon quern stone, St Mary le Port.* Courtesy of Prof. P. Rahtz

continuity and survival as subsequent periods took over and changed and modified the monuments of their ancestors.

Other remains of Anglo-Saxon stonework in Bristol include the masonry patterns of possible Saxon date carved into the wall of Glebe House parsonage at All Saints' Church in the city itself, and a fragment of interlace now built into the porch of Lawrence Weston farm. At the far end of Swinehead hundred, the former minster church at Bitton, endowed with 1 hide of land by the time of Edward the Confessor, still retains some features of the original Saxon church. These include an arch in the north wall, now filled in, which would have led to a chapel, and the feet of an Anglo-Saxon rood on the east end of the chancel near the roof. The rest of the sculpture was lost when the original high roof was lowered.

Turning aside from the churches, Bristol's buildings were almost entirely of timber: the home or workshop excavated along the 'hollow way' near St Mary le Port church was of wood, as were the buildings excavated on the Castle site and Tower Lane. The wooden workshops on the Tower Lane site had been pulled down in the twelfth century and a stone building constructed over them. The evidence for the timber buildings on the Castle site is mostly only suggestive of what the buildings may have looked like. Much was destroyed when the castle was built, and damage from burrowing animals, worms and tree roots had destroyed or obscured much of the evidence in the soil. Rather more could be said of the timber building by St Mary le Port, though even here things were not at all clear. It is however amazing that any evidence has survived. Aside from the clearances associated with the castle's construction, buildings in this period had a very short lifespan, 5-25 years, and planked flooring may have required replacing every 5-10. Needless to say, where buildings were of mostly timber and thatch, fire was an ever-present threat that could easily gut whole neighbourhoods. There could be considerable continuity in the town's plan, however. Although individual buildings could be destroyed or pulled down fairly regularly, the positions of the buildings remained constant. In Coppergate in York the position of the tenements remained unchanged for 50 years, through several bouts of fire damage and normal wear and tear.

The excavation of the timber building at the Castle site was incomplete, and so unlike the timber building in St Mary le Port Street, no plan could be drawn up. There is enough evidence from all three sites in the city, however, to draw a number of interesting conclusions about them and for a reasonable reconstruction of the buildings' structures to be made. All of the Saxon building techniques seem to have been used in Bristol. A number of post-holes were found at Tower Lane. Both the Castle and St Mary le Port buildings had post- and stake-holes, and a padstone for supporting the foundations was also found in the latter, as well as indications of the seating for upright planks and timber slots, which may have held short sill beams. This was a beam placed horizontally in the foundation trench or the surface of the building site to support the wall posts. A sill-beam laid directly on the ground was certainly found at the Castle site, which although now known from other sites, was unique when found.

Although the posts on the Castle site may have been used to support wattle and daub walls, the evidence for this in St Mary le Port Street is quite limited. Impressions from the wattle and laths do exist, as do indications of daub, but the building here seems to have been mostly constructed of posts and planks. It also had two posts serving as doorjambs set 1m apart from each other in the middle of the north wall, and which may have looked onto the emplacement for a wooden threshold. On the street outside were several deposits of slag, white limestone and charcoal, covered with blackened slabs of pennant sandstone, one of which, again, had on its surface fused slag. This was probably not waste from the blacksmithing being carried out at the site so much as deliberately placed there to raise the level of the surrounding street and provide a continuous, consolidated surface for the 'hollow way', the road running past the structure.

Metal slag was thrown as rubbish in pits at Tower Lane. At the back of the building, in its south-east corner, was a cess pit. Several slabs of pennant sandstone were used to form the exit for a drain running from this to the north-east corner of the building onto the street outside. The same stone also provided the packing for several of the post-holes. A number of cess pits were also found at Tower Lane, indicating that the citizens were keenly aware of this universal human need when building their dwellings. If the doorway at the St Mary le Port building was in the centre of the north wall, as believed, and the cess pit marked the south-east corner of the building, then it may have been about 4m wide by 6m long, with the shortest walls being the north and south ends of the structure. The buildings at Castle park may have been of similar dimensions, with a probable width of about 4m and 3.8m respectively, although the larger building had narrow extensions with thinner walls.

The main difference between the Castle, Tower Lane and St Mary le Port Street buildings seems to have been in the occupiers' attitude to fire. All three sites were used for metalworking, but only in the building at St Mary le Port Street is there evidence of an internal hearth. This was an area near the western end of the building composed of slabs of pennant sandstone set in the marl surface and covered with wood ash and soil mixed with charcoal. Although at the Castle site there were a number of stake-holes found around the forge stone, suggesting there was some kind of building around that, the furnace itself was outside the building associated with it, in the open air. In none of the buildings at the Castle site were any signs of internal hearths. This is not unusual in late Saxon buildings. The cooking fires may have been confined to braziers or upper floors. As fire was an ever-present threat, it shows that these early Bristolians were, by their standards at least, quite safety conscious. All the buildings show, moreover, that Bristolians did not lag behind the advances in building techniques being used in other eleventh-century English towns.

Although there is no direct evidence of it, there is the distinct possibility that eleventh-century Bristolians, like their modern descendants, kept gardens. Early charters from the ninth and tenth centuries describe individual plots in Canterbury and Rochester either as *hagas*, hedges, or *tuns*, in its original sense of enclosure. The term also appears in the *Domesday Book* for these cities as *hagae*, a latinised version of the Old English *haga* or *gehaeg*. This suggests that each plot was surrounded by a hedge, which in time became synonymous with the concept of an urban tenement. There is, however, a similar term, *haia*, used in the Midland shires, which had a different meaning, similarly derived from *haga* or *gehaeg*, and is cognate with the modern English place-name element *hay* and the French *haie*. Here the term means a three-sided hedged enclosure into which game was driven and caught. The meaning is made explicit in the entries for various estates in Shropshire, which state that *hays* were for the capture of roedeer. As few people hunt animals by driving them into their back gardens, it seems that these *hays* were set apart some distance from the town, and were therefore certainly neither gardens nor urban plots. A *hay* could also be the hawthorne hedge which fenced off certain pieces of woodland.

The similarity of both terms and their derivations suggests that it was only in Canterbury and Rochester that hedged plots were a common feature of the townscape. This does not, however, mean that agriculture may not have been practised within Bristol. There was no clear difference at this time between town and country. The citizens of a town held and cultivated land beyond its walls, and agriculture extended into the town itself. It is therefore entirely consistent that these *hays* belonged to the citizens of what was then a thriving metropolis. Many citizens kept pigs on their urban plots, for example. Some houses in Viking Dublin, and no doubt other Viking settlements elsewhere, did possess gardens. In Dublin these were confined to the homes along Fishamble Street. The irregular plots of land of the houses along Dublin's High Street suggests that Viking Dublin may have differed from Bristol in growing piecemeal over time. Bristol's grid pattern suggests planning, and the planners may not have envisaged gardening as one of the citizens' activities. Nevertheless, the fifteenth-century houses along Castle Park had herb gardens stretching down to the river, possibly following a precedent made 400 years earlier. Even if these plots were not developed for agriculture, they may still have been marked off from their neighbours by either hedges, or by fences and ditches, as in the cases of York and Thetford respectively. Traces of a fence have been found on the opposite side of St Mary le Port Street facing the timber building, which seems to have had some type of passage running past its western end. In addition to being used as building material for the houses, wattle was also used to line and build up the cess pits, in order to turn them into privies.

Outside of Bristol proper, evidence for a timber building in Bedminster comes from a slot trench cut into the natural sandstone at St John's Street/

Sheene Road. Evidence of occupation, but not necessarily habitation, comes from the remains of three Anglo-Saxon cemeteries excavated at St James' Priory, St Augustine the Less, and Westbury College. Above a possible boundary ditch on the Priory site were found 11 human burials, unusually aligned west-south-west to east-south-east rather than the east to west alignment commonly found in Christian inhumations. These graves had niches cut for the heads and ledges down the long sides of the graves, though not at the feet. The lack of coffins and accompanying nails suggest that the corpses were only buried in their shrouds. Similar head niche graves were found at St Augustine the Less, where six adult burials were discovered dating from the eleventh century, with radiocarbon testing dating them to 1070. Of these, two were buried in cist graves, while another was a body-shaped grave with a niche cut for the head and shoulders. Like the burials at St James', these too were unusually aligned, though this timenorth-west to south-east, possibly due to a building, boundary marker or road, which has not survived. There are obvious parallels with similar burials dating from the eleventh or twelfth century at St Mary's, Rivenhall, in Essex, while side ledges are an Anglo-Saxon feature. It is not known what their purpose was. Explanations have included the possibility that they were cut to support a covering slab, though the lack of similar ledges at the feet would seem to make this unlikely. Apart from Bristol, they are also known from a cemetery in Kent dated to the seventh or eighth century.

Excavations of the burial site at Westbury College, however, yielded only one complete male skeleton, though fragments of human bone were recovered from pits elsewhere in the cemetery. The remains of a timber building were also found, along with a stone jetty and riverside wall against the Trym. Unfortunately, there was insufficient evidence to date the remains, so that they could come from any point in time from between the late seventh or (more likely) early eighth century, and the twelfth. While it is tempting to see these as being evidence for the early monastic buildings there, they could just as well be wholly or partly the remains of secular buildings put up during the intervening years of Viking devastation and secular usurpation.

# 5 Trade and industry

Although Bristol's location on the tidal shores of the Severn and Avon gave Bristol excellent river and marine communications with Ireland, South Wales, southern and mid-England and the European Atlantic coast, documentary evidence for trade is scant, largely coming from twelfth-century chroniclers such as William of Malmesbury and Richard of Devizes. It is only from the thirteenth century that detailed records of the scale and nature of Bristolian trading begin to appear. Nevertheless, archaeological evidence, commercial clauses in later charters (such as that of Henry II of 1155), and incidents recorded by the twelfth-century monastic chroniclers give some indication of the type of goods traded by Bristol, and the identity of her trading partners.

Seven hundred years before Bristol exploited black slaves from Africa, it was notorious for its part in the trade of human beings to Ireland. It was this traffic that brought the ire of the great Anglo-Saxon divine, Bishop Wulfstan, upon the city. The citizens of Bristol were infamous for buying English slaves, or worse, offering up for sale to the Norse merchants women whom they had themselves made pregnant. To combat this, Wulfstan would take up residence in the city for three months at a time, preaching against it every Sunday. By the end of his episcopacy, his preaching had had an effect. Any slaver caught was blinded and driven out of the city, and the trade itself was banned. Although the slave trade was outlawed in 1100, slavery itself was not abolished, and it seems that the trade itself merely went underground. Thirteen years after its formal abolition a party of nine canons, collecting funds for the rebuilding of Laon Cathedral, spent two nights aboard an Irish merchant ship in Bristol docks. Warned by their host that the Irish were in the habit of getting people aboard their ships, and then sailing away with them to sell to barbarians, the canons cancelled a third visit. Trading with the Irish was obviously profitable, but hazardous.

According to William of Malmesbury, Wulfstan was able to win the Bristolians over against the trade after his image miraculously appeared to the crew of a Bristolian vessel wrecked adrift during the voyage to Ireland. This vision gave the instructions necessary to repair the ship and reach safe harbour in Ireland, returning with fair winds. Although modern scepticism casts considerable doubt on the story, especially given the medieval reputation for credulity and superstition, also notorious among mariners, the tale does show the immense importance of seafaring trade to eleventh-century Bristolians, and an awareness amongst the Worcestershire clergy that to establish their moral authority there, at least as regards the slave trade, they had to prove their spiritual prowess not only in the realm of morals, but also over the physically treacherous weather of the Irish Sea.

Things other than slaves were traded with the Irish. In the twelfth century Bristolians imported a number of foodstuffs from the Emerald Isle, as well as timber, cloth (such as the famous Irish linen), and hides for the city's leather industry. In return Bristol exported iron, salt, fine English cloth and worked leather products. Bristolians also re-exported imported articles like spice. England had a reputation for fine quality wool and needlework throughout the Anglo-Saxon period, and the city certainly had a leather industry, so it is possible that the origins of the trade in these commodities lay in the eleventh century. From Dublin, goods could be re-exported throughout the Viking world, even as far as Iceland, where in AD 1000 a merchant vessel arrived with a cargo of bedclothes: beautifully embroidered English sheets, a silken quilt and other valuable goods, which were rare in Iceland. Perhaps the bedclothes had first been exported to Ireland from Bristol. The dedication to St Werburgha of that church may be an indication of the strength of the trade links with Ireland even then.

Too much stress can be laid on the Irish connection, however. The channel allowed Bristolians to trade with a number of regions and peoples aside from the Irish. William of Malmesbury noted that in his time ships came to Bristol not just from Ireland, but from Norway among other countries, and there is little reason to doubt that Norwegian traders visited Bristol earlier in the previous century. The Severn also gave Bristolians easy access to ports further up the coast, such as Gloucester. Gloucester was the centre of a vigorous iron industry, the products of which the Bristolian smiths would have been eager to enjoy. There is no evidence of metal smelting in Bristol, so it seems that the local smiths imported their iron from outside. Given Gloucester's relative closeness and ease of access, it would be surprising if that city were not this outside source.

From the historian's point of view, the other most important trade in Bristol was the mint, as this allows us to make some estimation of the city's age and importance. Thanks to the nature of the product, we even know the names of the people involved. Until the reign of Edward I, the moneyers stamped their names and that of their mint, in this case Bristol, on their coins. The moneyers Aelfweard, Aegelwine, and Aelfwine were active throughout the Anglo-Saxon period, being joined at times by others such as Leofwine, Wulstan, Saewine, Wulnoth, Aelwig, Aethestan, Aelfric, Smeawine and Ceorl. Even the traumatic events of the Norman Conquest had little effect on this trade, as William I left the mints in the hands of the experienced Saxon moneyers already working. Until the major changes of Henry II's reign, most of the moneyers came from families of English or Danish descent. Bristol was no exception: Ceorl and Leofwine continued working under the Conqueror. Other English moneyers who began working in his reign included Brunstan,

Brihtword and Colblac. As further evidence of Bristol's Scandinavian connections, some of the moneyers after the Conquest, such as Swegn, had Viking names. Their tenure of the mint was entirely undisturbed, however. The Bristol moneyer Herthig was amongst those in 1124 who were threatened with the amputation of their right hand, and 'the loss of the lower parts of their bodies' in the decorous phrase of Florence of Worcester for the debasement of the coinage. Despite this Herthig and his fellows remained in business for another ten years.

Unfortunately the location of the mint is unknown. Later Bristol coinage of the Tealby type, struck *c*.1158-80, was minted at the moneyers' workshops next to St Ewen's Church, the site of the Old Council House at the corner of Broad Street and Corn Street. Medieval local mints were always situated near, or in their town's busiest districts, and this area was long associated with the banking and financial heart of Bristol. It is reasonable to assume that continuity and tradition played an important part in siting the mint there, and that this was the location of the Saxon mint. During excavations at St Mary le Port Church in 1962-3 a coin dated to Harold II's reign was discovered, and this hints that the mint may well have been in that area.

Quite how many people were employed at the mint is unknown, but the total could have been considerable. In the mid-thirteenth century the mint employed four moneyers, four mint keepers, two goldsmiths, one clerk and at least 20 workmen. The staff of the Saxon mint was almost definitely smaller, but may still have been quite large. The mint and its staff are omitted from the *Domesday Book*, which seems strange considering it was compiled to assess England's economic productivity. The Bristol mint was not alone in being excluded: several other mints were similarly left out.

All the coins minted during the Anglo-Saxon period in Bristol were silver pennies, which were of far too high a denomination to be used for normal business in the market. For most of their normal trade Bristolians probably bartered. In form, the coinage struck remained constant. On the obverse was a portrait of the reigning king, his name in Latin and the formula *Rex Anglorum*: 'King of the English'. The reverse bore a decorative pattern, the name of the moneyer and the site of the mint, prefaced by *on*, meaning 'in'. Bristol was usually shortened to '*Bric*', so that, for example, the reverse of a coin of Aelfwine could read '*Aelfwine On Bric*'. This '*On Bric*' legend can be deceptive: other candidates for that legend in the tenth century are Bridgnorth in Shropshire and Stockbridge in Hampshire, and it is possible that the coin of Aethelred II considered as possibly showing existence of the mint during his reign actually refers instead to Bridgnorth. Coins produced by the moneyer Godwine, coming at the end of Edward the Confessor's reign, are much less ambiguous, however. These sometimes render the town's name as *Bricsto* or *Brvcsto*.

Many other trades and activities were going on in Bristol, as well as slave trading and minting. One trade common to nearly every Anglo-Saxon

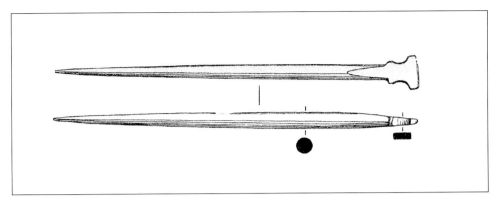

**22** *Viking-style pins, St Mary le Port.* Courtesy of Prof. P. Rahtz

settlement, whether village or *burh*, was that of the blacksmith. People depended on him not just for the manufacture and maintenance of their tools, but for weapons, armour and even the jewellery and pins that secured their clothing. Excavations of St Mary le Port Church and its street revealed that the timber house might also have served as a metal worker's workshop. Iron ore, slag, bits of crucible and white limestone and charcoal were found in it, extending into the road outside. One wall held the remains of a possible furnace. Elsewhere in the street, deposits of lead and a copper alloy clothes fastener were discovered, while under the Castle, deposits of white ash and charcoal were found, indicating extensive iron-working activity. Remains of a timber building were discovered, outside of which was a large area of burnt clay and ash, which served as the furnace for the smiths. To the east of this was a forge stone still in its original position (although broken), which when reconstructed was roughly circular in shape. The stake holes surrounding the stone indicate that it was probably insulated from the heat by a structure using a thick layer of clay. Similar stones found in Scandinavia suggest that the stone's purpose was to protect the bellows from the heat when blowing into the furnace. The furnace itself was shallow. Like the hearth and furnace in St Mary le Port Street, it seems to have been used for smithing, for the manufacture and repair of tools and other objects, rather than smelting. Similarly, an amount of iron slag was also found during excavations of Tower Lane, indicating that metalworking was carried on there too. The position of the rubbish pits in which it was discovered suggested that the timber workshops associated with it were closer to the main road, which may have followed the present course of Broad Street.

There is a wealth of ceramic material from Saxon and medieval Bristol. Excavations at Peter Street, Tower Lane, St Mary le Port Street and Castle Park have all uncovered examples of Anglo-Saxon pottery. This should not be too surprising, as Bristol was one of the major pottery centres throughout the Middle Ages with its Ham Green Ware, and the porcelain and glass-making industries flourished in the seventeenth and eighteenth centuries. The Saxon finds contained several fragments of cooking pots, each having a slightly different fabric. The first cooking pot was of a type which had an upright, flat-topped, but clubbed rim, and which sagged at the base. There was a very strong angle to the shoulders and neck. The clay of which it was composed was light and grey, porous and pitted where fragments of limestone and shell were leached or burnt out. It seems to have been thrown on a wheel, but the speed appears to have been quite slow and the pot was finished by hand. One of the pots found at Bristol Castle showed signs of being built up in coils without a wheel, as many primitive pots are still done today. The second type of cooking pot was distinguished by having a simple rim, with a slack profile and no angle at the shoulder and neck. Internally, it was slightly concave. Again, it had a sagging base, or at least a base which lacked the normal angles. It had suffered some oxidation during firing. The clay also had a bumpy surface and contained grey limestone and quartz. The third type of pot followed the second in appearance and type of clay, but had rather more quartz than limestone, and was pitted. A possible variant of this type of pot was fired hard, and heavily oxidised, even to the very centre of the fabric.

There was also a number of handmade cooking pots with simple rims and smooth surfaces, but containing a large number of quartz fragments, which were often coloured and rounded. These pots are very similar to the CC type of pottery found at Cheddar. Other cooking pots had a black or grey fabric, which contained much flint or quartz, some of which could be as large as three millimetres and coloured, but with little chalk. The presence of soft limestone and shell indicates that the clay at least came from the Cotswolds, while that of coloured quartz points to an origin in Somerset. Rose quartz is a common feature of the Ilchester area pottery of Cheddar CC type. The Cheddar pottery in turn was similar to Portchester area pottery, though the sagging base seems to have been a feature local to the south-west. The pots found at St Mary le Port Street were similar to this, though pots of the A fabric appear here earlier than at the Castle site. A type pottery were hand-worked bowls and pots of a sandy fabric, hard fired, with calcareous and quartz fragments and occasional red flecks. On the Castle site they have been dated to around 1080-1150. Elsewhere in Bristol, at St Mary le Port, Peter Street and Westbury College, they appear much earlier, perhaps the late tenth to early eleventh centuries. Perhaps the new Norman lords in their castle took rather longer to get used to the local craftsmen.

The potters in Bristol did not confine themselves to making eating vessels. They also produced small oil lamps, such as those found on the Castle site and in St Mary le Port Street. Those from St Mary le Port were about 2.3-4.7in (6-12cm) in diameter at the top, narrowing to bases about 1.9in (5cm) in diameter. The intact lamps stood about 2.3-2.7in (6-7cm) tall. The example found at the Castle had a red to grey surface, a form which differed from other lamps found at Cheddar. As only a sherd was recovered it is regrettably unknown whether it rested on a spike or a stand such as those at Cheddar.

The bases of similar lamps found elsewhere were splayed so that they could be set on the floor or in a niche on the wall.

Other items of Bristolian pottery recovered include a Saxo-Norman shard recovered from Church Lane near St Peter's Church. Outside of the core area of Bristol, Anglo-Saxon pottery has also been recovered from the medieval waterfront at Bridge Parade, and the remains of a thirteenth-century house excavated at Stockwood. The Stockwood finds included one shard of the body of a wheel-stamped coarseware pot, of a type found at St Mary le Port Street. The pot here was handmade with a red surface, the clay mixed with limestone, fossil shell and haematite, and pitted where some of these inclusions have leached out and a rim and neck shard of a later, though related ware used in cooking pots also found at Bristol Castle from *c*.1070-1100. Like its predecessor, this has a red surface, though it is more finely finished with finer and more evenly distributed inclusions. There were also eight shards of a pottery of a darker fabric, though with an occasional reddish surface and containing quartz, haematite and limestone, also of a later eleventh- to early twelfth-century date and found at Bristol Castle, along with a single shard of a quartz gritted fabric containing inclusions of up to 1mm in size, resembling some of the tripod pitchers believed to come from Wiltshire. It is possible that this ware was glazed. The Redcliffe material also included shards of pottery dating from *c*.1080, one type of which ceased production by the early twelfth century.

In addition, Bristol seemed to be the centre for a leather-working industry. Goat and sheep offcuts were found at St Mary le Port Street, along with an awl, which had been thrown into the cess pit serving the timber building. Horners' workshops also catered for the city. In the hollow way passing outside of St Mary le Port Church were found a number of horn cores from cattle, sheep, goats and pigs, suggesting that the horns had been removed and worked, although in the case of the goats the horns sometimes remained in place. Although the horner has been made obsolete by the invention of plastic, he was an important craftsman in the Middle Ages. Bone, horn and antler supplied the material for caskets, pins, strap ends, sword mounts and other items. They also made bone combs, remains of three of which were also found, and which appear to have been rejects broken during manufacture. Animal bones were found in the rubbish pits at Tower Lane, which may point to bone-working being carried on there too, although this may, on the other hand, be waste from a slaughterhouse or butchers.

Spinning was also carried out in Bristol, the main evidence being a set of seven pottery and sandstone spindle whorls, from St Mary le Port Street, Tower Lane and one from the Castle. Those from St Mary le Port were stone, 1.1-1.33in (30-4mm) in diameter and 0.7-1.3in (18-33mm) in height. They had all been turned on a lathe. The example from Tower Lane was made of pottery, perhaps because suitable stone was either unavailable or too expensive. Spinning and weaving were domestic activities rather than an industry in the Anglo-Saxon period. Eleventh-century women had to spin, weave and sew the clothes for their families.

The spindle whorls also provide a clue to another industry carried out in Bristol: quarrying. In the opinion of Dr Vince, at least one, and possibly several, of the stone whorls found at St Mary le Port Street was made from calcite mudstone, which was available around Bristol. Thus, the whorls may have been just one product of a large local industry. The example from Castle Park was made of Pennant Sandstone, which may also have been quarried nearby. In addition to the stone, sand seems to have been quarried in the city. The rubbish pits at Tower Lane, for example, appear to have been excavated for their sand, probably for making the mortar, which covered the churches and possibly several other buildings in the city. Other shallow pits suggesting sand digging have been found at St John's Street/Sheene Road in Bedminster, and Peter Street, probably for use in building the Norman town wall and Castle. Lastly, as we have seen, lead was mined on the Downs in Clifton.

# 6  Agriculture and food

It may appear strange to include a chapter on agriculture in a book about a town, but to the medievals it would have made perfect sense. The Anglo-Saxon word *tun*, from which the modern English word 'town' is derived, could mean estate or dwelling, as well as village. Its primary meaning was 'enclosure'. The division between town and countryside was not as sharp then as it is now. Towns were an innovation in a primarily agricultural economy, and not clearly differentiated from the farms around them. About 95 per cent of the English population worked on the land, and every town throughout the Middle Ages was surrounded by an area of farmland owned and worked by the burgesses. When Alfred set up the *burhs* in the late ninth century, he passed laws providing a certain amount of land to each *burh* for its support and defence. These amounts were calculated on the formula of 16 hides per acre's breadth or 22 yards of wall. This gradual merging of town and countryside means that the Anglo-Saxon *burhware* or burgess should not be immediately identified with the modern concept of a town's citizen who lives within a particular town or city, earning his or her living by trade or industrial labour. The Anglo-Saxon *burhwaru* were those citizens who were responsible for the borough customs, even though they may actually have lived outside the town itself.

During the excavation of St Mary le Port Street, around 1,500 animal bones were found scattered along the remains of a twelfth-century road, the hollow way. These bones seemed to be waste from a slaughterhouse and butcher's shop, rather than private household rubbish. Most of the animals seem to have been sheep, followed by cattle then goats and pigs. There are even some dog and cat bones, which may well have been the remains of household pets, strays that had become a nuisance, or indicate that they had been eaten during times of famine. Fragments of bone from horses were also found. The church banned the eating of horseflesh because of its connections with paganism and the cult of the Viking god Freyr, so the likelihood is that these were working animals which had come to the end of their life, or that the had been eaten only out of dire necessity during a time of starvation.

The number of cattle finds should not be surprising. A law passed at the end of the tenth century stated that oxen could only be slaughtered in the presence of two witnesses. Towns thus became the obvious place for their slaughter. Cattle bones are the commonest animal remains on all Viking Age sites, whether settled by the Norsemen or not, and beef and dairy products were part of the staple diet throughout England. Indeed, the overall amounts of the different animals eaten in Bristol, as estimated from these bones, are the same as other places in the eleventh century, with one exception: the number of pigs consumed is exceptionally low. Although they were the only type of food animal which could be kept in towns, being reared and fattened in wattle pens, pigs did suffer from a serious disadvantage: unlike cattle, sheep and goats, which can supply milk, hides for tanning and, in the case of sheep, wool, pigs only provide meat. It thus makes little economic sense to rear them, compared to the other animals. On the other hand, they could fend for themselves and eat scraps, and when slaughtered the amount of fat and pork provided by only one pig would last a family through the winter. The answer perhaps lies in religious convictions. Although Christianity had long thrown off the dietary restrictions of the *Old Testament*, some Anglo-Saxons kept them through religious zeal: the fisherman in Aelfric's *Colloquy on the Professions* would not eat shellfish, for example.

All these animals might have come from the hinterland around Bristol, though the cattle could have been driven from as far away as Wales. The great cattle drives across the border were in existence even then, and went far beyond Bristol. Mixed up in the animal bones were those of a small number of birds, including goosander and widgeon. These were waterfowl, which probably had been caught in the autumn or winter.

Most of the cattle slaughtered were young, around one and a half to four years old. This is too young for the animals to have reached maturity and realised their value as prime cuts. Animals were far slower maturing in the Middle Ages, and even in the latter part of the nineteenth century, when methods of cattle feeding were improving and the animals were bred for early maturity, it was considered that an animal should be at least five years old before it reached its best. Meat was therefore an expensive food. The young age of the animals suggest they were deliberately slaughtered at an early age to supply meat, possibly during a shortage or simply because there was a demand for cheap meat. The lack of good joints and small bones among the finds indicates that the site was probably a retail butcher's, rather than a wholesale abattoir. Mutton and lamb, unlike beef, is sold on the bone; the small bones taken away with the joints from sheep were likely to be thrown away on small local rubbish heaps serving individual households. The young age of the animals being slaughtered in Bristol matches a pattern emerging elsewhere in the country during the eleventh century. Although sheep in Flaxengate were only slaughtered after they had served a long career as a provider of wool and milk, the younger animals again were increasingly selected for slaughter. At York the animals were butchered between the ages of 18 months and four years; this means that some were being kept specifically as meat animals, while others were being killed after one year's woolclip.

These bones give an indication of the size and breed of the animals bred by the Anglo-Saxons. The cattle, sheep, horses and pigs were much smaller than those of modern breeds. The animals' lack of height was due to non-selective breeding carried on from Neolithic times. In addition to their lack of size, Viking Age pigs had relatively longer legs than modern animals, and were hairier and darker skinned, with prick ears and short bodies. The cattle found in Bristol were extremely small, more so than their counterparts in Lund in the Netherlands and parts of south Germany. Although taller than the Iron Age animals, they were still smaller than the modern Chillingham breeds. It seems the animals were at the lowest viable limit of their height.

The horn cores recovered also give some indication of what the animal may have looked like. Most of the cores were of a moderate length and bent upwards, so that the animals may have looked something like the modern Ayrshire (although predating this by several hundred years). One horn was strongly curved forward like contemporary Dutch cattle or Celtic shorthorn, while another specimen was turned backwards. Yet another horn was noted for its strong spiral grooves.

The sheep bones and horn cores in Bristol again demonstrate the small size of the sheep in this period, and also suggest that the animals had been horned before slaughter. The animals' slender bones suggest a type like the Soay sheep, a breed similar to wild sheep. Soay sheep also have the advantage from the weavers' point of view that the fleeces can be pulled off the animal quite easily without resorting to shearing. Bristolians and their neighbours, however, do not seem to have confined themselves to keeping just one type. One horn found seems to have belonged to an animal similar to the modern short-tailed Heath breed, while another appeared to have belonged to a genus where the horns of the male grow round in a complete circle. There was also evidence of sexual dimorphism. This is when the male and female of a species are very different from each other in appearance. One horn from a male animal was grooved on its medial surface, but the horn from the female was smooth with a hole at the rear base. This also occurred in the eighth-century animals kept in Norfolk, and in modern breeds such as the Scottish Blackface and Norfolk Horn.

Most of the goat horns found were male. The animals were large horned, and similar to the goats kept in other parts of the British Isles. Although this type of goat nearly became extinct in the nineteenth century when large numbers of Swiss goats were imported, the breed still survives in the wild in parts of Scotland. In this respect, Bristol was quite remarkable, as in other parts of the country around this time, such as York, goats were kept mostly as dairy animals, so were predominantly female.

It is nearly impossible to describe the type of pig farmed around Bristol, because of the small numbers of bones found and the extremely early age the animals were slaughtered. It would be reasonable to say, however, that they were probably small versions of the wild pigs depicted in much medieval liter-ature. Modern British breeds arose only in the eighteenth century, when native breeds were bred with animals imported from China. Recently there have been attempts to breed the original Iron Age animal again, by crossing a Red Tamworth sow with a wild boar. When born, the piglets were dark brownish grey with stripes of grey fawn colour. Surprisingly, given the fearsome reputation of wild boars, they were actually quite docile and tame.

Although the *Domesday Book* does not mention the number and type of animals in Bristol, some idea of the livestock raised in the area can be found in its pages. The entries for Bedminster, Knowle and Keynsham all list the type of animals raised on these manors. From this it appears that the area was a predominantly sheep farming region. Sheep represent 80.69 per cent of the animals raised, although most of these were the massive flock of 700 sheep grazing on the Keynsham estate. Cattle accounted for only 2.6 per cent of the animal population, goats 6.9, and pigs 9 per cent. Cobs, presumably the short-legged riding horses, although possibly male swans, constituted about half of the animals being reared. Within the Keynsham estate itself, most of the stock was concentrated on the royal demesne land. At Keynsham proper, 77.7 per cent of the sheep were raised, if the 9.6 per cent of sheep belonging to Aelfric are included with those specifically mentioned as stationed on the Keynsham estate, which composed 67.6 per cent of the sheep population. Burnett, Stanton and Belluton accounted for 9.6, 8.4, and 4.5 per cent of the sheep population respectively. Keynsham also held most of the manor's goat population. It held 70 of the animals, with the estate's other ten at Belluton. Keynsham also had 44 pigs, Belluton 13 and Burnett six. The area's cattle population was split evenly between Keynsham and Belluton, both settlements holding ten each.

The meadowland held by the estate was similarly dominated by Keynsham proper. Keynsham possessed 100 (40.46ha) of the 155 acres (62.75ha) of meadowland on the manor, 117 (47.3ha) if Aelfric's property is counted with it. Belluton, Stanton and Burnett had only 22, 15 and 12 acres (8.9, 6, and 4.85ha) respectively. The manor's pasturage was divided in similar proportions. Belluton had 20 and Stanton 60 acres (8 and 24.29ha) each, while Keynsham had 100 acres (40.48ha), though Aelfric in this instance merely contributed an additional 2 acres (0.8ha). Keynsham was also well provided for regarding woodland: 1000 acres (404.85ha) were spread over the main estate, with Stanton and Belluton each possessing 60 acres (24.29ha).

While this suggests that Bedminster and Keynsham, the areas both marked as sheep-rearing land, were the source of so many of the sheep eaten in Bristol, it also raises other unanswered questions. The *Domesday Book* does not count the animal resources on each manor, except plough teams, which it considers as a measure of arable land. Other parts of the survey do include livestock, but only for restricted parts of the country, and tend to ignore those owned by *villeins*. Much of the land held in the area, even after the Conquest, was the property of ridingmen, *radcnihts*. They needed horses for their duties, but these are not listed. The barons and Norman knights certainly took an interest in stock rearing, even if many of the knights could not afford a charger of their own. So where are they? No oxen are listed in Barton Regis, like so many other places, though the peasants must obviously have ploughed with them. Clearly, the *Domesday Book* is far less comprehensive than the list of all the livestock, down to the last ox, cow and pig lamented by the Laud chronicler for 1085.

On a more domestic level, parts of two Anglo-Saxon quernstones were found in the hollow way in St Mary le Port Street. These were common domestic items in the Saxon period, with almost every household having one. These two in Bristol were made of Old Red Sandstone, which is available around Bristol and so possibly adds further corroboration quarrying in the area. They are unusual because the favoured stone for querns was Niedermendig lava from Germany. They were both upper stones from a handmill.

Aside from these handmills, the Anglo-Saxons also used watermills to grind their meal. Bristolians may have been well-served in this regard: the *Domesday Book* records that Barton Regis possessed two mills valued at 27 shillings, a not inconsiderable sum. Bedminster also had a mill, as did the villages in Brentry, which they had to share. Keynsham was blessed with six. Although no remains have been found, the mill pool at Stoke Bishop is still visible. Generally, mills all over Europe were located close to bridges, and so it is only to be expected that Bristol, or at least Barton Regis, should have possessed several.

The 22 villagers of Barton Regis mentioned in the *Domesday Book* were *villeins*. These were a new class emerging by the time of the Norman Conquest, formed from free farmers on the one hand gradually becoming

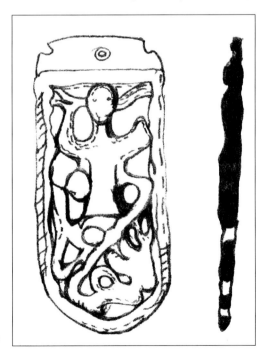

**23** *The Winterbourne strap-end.* After J. Stewart

depressed into serfdom, and from freed slaves, *coliberti*, on the other gradually acquiring more freedom. The *villeins* themselves were bound to the soil and their property escheated to their lords at their deaths. The term *villein* is vague, however, and denoted several different types of half-free farmer. Some of the *villeins* were undoubtedly closer to the Saxon *geneats* and *ceorls*, who both had their own lands in addition to those they held for their lords. In some parts of the *Domesday Book* the term *villanus* is used to describe high-status farmers such as *radcnihts*, who occupied a position well beyond that of an agricultural labourer. In most instances in the *Domesday Book* however the term merely implies a farmer who held land according to the traditional shares of his village: that of a yardland, half-yardland, even a hide or, more likely, a half-hide.

The term *villanus*, *villein*, thus was simply used by the Normans to describe the commonest type of villager, with little regard for the niceties of individual status. Nevertheless, most *villeins* seem to have been the equivalent of the Anglo-Saxon *geburs*. These were freedmen who occupied a farm. There was very little difference between them and medieval *villeins*. The *geburs* were better off than the slaves; they had certain rights, and could not be punished with the lash, although they were still liable to plead in their local lord's court rather than in the hundred courts.

Below the *villeins* in the *Domesday Book* are the *bordarii*, smallholders, or *cottarii*, cottagers, or to use the Anglo-Saxon term, *cotsetlan*. They were similar to the *villeins*, but humbler. Their holdings were smaller than those of the *geburs*, but there seemed to be a minimum area with which it was considered his lord should provide him. In status they were similar to the hutted serfs of the Roman Empire, and many of them may have been manumitted slaves. Their own smallholdings would not have been sufficient either to support them or occupy all of their time, so that they probably performed other services for their lord or the richer *villeins* in return for wages. If the *Domesday Book* as a whole is examined, it seems that the disturbances during 1066 and afterwards had been hard on the *geburs*. Many of them were already sinking into the *cotsetla* class. The social framework in which they fell is, however, English, and not entirely the imposition of a foreign king.

The *Domesday Book* also mentions a group of *coliberti*, or freedmen. These were a class of men who had been former slaves and emancipated in groups. In the *Domesday Book* they mostly appear in Wessex and parts of Mercia, suggesting that they may have partly been remnants of the indigenous British population who were enslaved by the invading English. Even though they were now free, making up part of the *gebur* class, their unfree origins still seem to have been held against them, for they are classed separately to the other *geburs*. This seems to be the case in Gloucestershire, though elsewhere in the *Domesday Book* there are two notes stating that the *coliberti* were also known as *bures*, or *buri* — i.e. *geburs*. Where the *coliberti* seem to differ from the rest of the *gebur* class is that the *coliberti*, although technically free, were in law still tied to their former masters, but not the estates on which they had been settled.

Far below these peasants in the social scale were the slaves, *servi* (male) and *ancillae* (female), for which the Old English term was *theow*, or the new Norse loan-word, *thraell*. In the tenth century, up to a quarter of the population was probably slaves, though because of their ubiquity and lack of importance in the social hierarchy it is difficult to estimate the exact numbers. Nevertheless, although lacking land of their own, the slaves did enjoy certain privileges. They were entitled to be fed by the lord when working for him, and received an allowance of money or kind for food.

The decline in slavery is not obvious in Barton Regis from its entry in the *Domesday Book*. Rather the opposite, in fact: the number of slaves had actually increased to nine in 1086, from the four recorded a generation previously. This, however, seems to be in line with the natural increase in the estate's population as a whole. There were five more *villeins* and one more smallholder in 1086, as opposed to 17 villagers and 24 smallholders in 1066. The 13 freedmen who held land there in 1066 had by the time of the *Domesday* survey increased by five. This growth in population seems to have been due to the tenants having children, or their children then coming of age and being counted as part of the adult, agricultural population. Mangotsfield, already a satellite of Bristol by virtue of its inclusion within the manor of Barton Regis, had a population of four smallholders and a ridingman. This was the *radcniht*, a member of the *geneat* class of free farmers, who amongst his other services was expected to ride on his lord's errands and keep guard over his lord and his stables. There was certainly nothing servile about him, and he lived a very good life compared to the mass of Saxon farmers.

Nevertheless, agricultural work, especially ploughing, was made particularly bitter by the fact that its workers were unfree. Ploughs were expensive items. Many of those used on the manors were held by the local lords. Barton Regis had three ploughs in lordship, which compares well with the regional average in the Bristol area of approximately 3.3. The small tenants who held their lands often had to club together to afford their ploughs. The *villeins* and smallholders of Barton Regis held 21 ploughs between them, while the four slaves and 13 freedmen had three. There were thus 24 ploughs in private hands on the estate, giving an average of nearly one plough between two peasants. The regional average was about one plough between 2.65 people, a strange figure which can be explained through the slaves, and possibly many freemen, on many estates not owning ploughs, and therefore presumably dependant on the ploughs held by their masters.

Not everyone was engaged in agricultural work. Aside from the miners themselves, the burgess mentioned at Pucklechurch may have been a merchant or some other tradesman, possibly connected with the mine. Some of the slaves may have had domestic or other duties, such as serving as falconers and oxherds for their lords, and so not been directly involved in ploughing. Several slaves in Thornbury are mentioned in connection with the mill, suggesting that their duties lay there, rather than on the land.

Nevertheless, ploughing was the most important and gruelling of the agricultural work, and the plough the most ubiquitous symbol of medieval England's agrarian nature.

Aside from this, some hundreds in the West Country chose September to elect their officers. Watchet Court Leet holds its Law Day on the old quarter day of Michaelmas, 29 September. Bristol's *Pied Poudre*, 'Dusty Feet', Court meets at the end of the month. Although a twelfth-century institution, created to supervise Bristol's markets and fairs, the date of its annual meeting is in line with Anglo-Saxon tradition regarding the dates for the rendering of rents and settlement of outstanding debts, and so may be a rough guide to when Barton Regis' hundred court met. Presumably the end of the month was chosen because by then the frenetic harvesting was over and the hundredors could take stock of the situation, perhaps literally regarding food stores, for the coming year.

This agricultural social structure was, unsurprisingly, typical of the other settlements surrounding Bristol. In Edric's former *fief* of Hanham, the *Domesday Book* records there were four slaves, eight smallholders and two ploughs held by the local lord. Bishopsworth, the possession of Geoffrey of Coutances by the time of the *Domesday Book*, had been held by two separate lords, Algar and Edric. Algar's territory included three slaves, two smallholders and ten houses in Bristol and two in Bath, though only a single plough was held by the lord himself. It was, though, furnished with 12 acres (4.85ha) of meadow, and a stretch of woodland 6 furlongs (1.1km) long by 1 furlong (183m) wide. Edric's division of the settlement contained four villagers, four smallholders and four cottars, with 10 acres (4ha) of meadow and 45 acres (18.22ha) of pasture.

Approaching Keynsham, Saltford was held before the Norman victory at Hastings by four *thegns*, members of the Anglo-Saxon nobility. Like Keynsham and Bedminster, it was predominantly a sheep-rearing community, with 120 animals recorded. It also boasted 13 pigs and one cob, with a mill and 32 acres (just under 13ha) of meadow. The population included seven *villeins* and ten smallholders who owned four ploughs, with another three held by the lord himself.

Knowle, on the other hand, was dedicated to swine and stock-rearing. A settlement of five *villeins* and six smallholders who held two ploughs, with another owned by the local lord, its 16 acres (6.48ha) of meadow, 20 acres (8.10ha) of pasture and two and a half furlongs (502.92m) of woodland supported 25 pigs, eight cattle and one cob. Prior to the Norman invasion, the landlord had been Alnoth 'the Constable', whose surname, from the Latin *comes stabuli*, 'Count of the Stables', suggests he may have had some role in rearing and caring for the local lord's horses. On the other hand, it may mean that he was or had been the steward of the local fortifications, the nearest and most obvious being those of Bristol. Could this imply that Alnoth had been the *thegn* responsible for the *burhbot*, the fortification and defence, of Bristol?

By the time of the *Domesday Book*, Knowle was a royal possession whose tenants held it directly from the king himself. It may well be that Alnoth was therefore involved in running the royal stud.

On the opposite side of Bristol, Clifton, with only 8 acres (3.23ha) of meadow and three ploughs held by the lord, supported a population of six *villeins*, six smallholders owning two ploughs, and three slaves. For Bristol's manor of Mangotsfield, in which 3 hides of land were held by the church, and six oxen and a plough by the local lord, the *Domesday Book* records there were four smallholders owning one plough, and a *radcniht* with a single hide of land and plough. *Radcnihts* were also important members of the population of Westbury on Trym. A group of six of them held eight hides and eight ploughs in the manor's individual communities of Henbury, Redwick, Stoke Bishop and Yate. Nine ploughs were held by the local lord, the rest of the population consisting of 27 *villeins*, 22 smallholders with 26 ploughs, 20 male and two female slaves and 20 freedmen with ten ploughs. The lands of St Mary's of Worcester, in contrast, retained two ploughs in lordship, supporting a population of eight *villeins* and six smallholders with eight ploughs, and four male and one female slave. Oldland, a former property of Harold's free man, Alfwy, of 10 acres (4.05ha) with a plough in lordship, had a population of six smallholders with a plough, one *villein* and two slaves. Hambrook, another of Algar's properties, with 6 acres (2.43ha) of meadow and two ploughs in lordship, had a population of two slaves, and two *villeins* who owned two ploughs between them.

Paradoxically, what emerges from this study of agricultural wealth is the immense importance of trade to the prosperity of Bristol. The manor was relatively small, merely 6 hides if the four at Mangotsfield is included, while Keynsham had 50, as did Westbury on Trym. Assuming that roughly 1 hide of land corresponded to an area of 120 acres (48.6ha), both Westbury and Keynsham occupied an area of about 6000 acres (2429ha) or about 9.9 square miles (15.6km). Bristol and Mangotsfield, on the other hand, were only 10 hides, about 1200 acres (485.8ha) or 1.87 square miles (2.9km). Keynsham had a population density of about ten people per square mile, (1.8km), a number which compares favourably with an average of seven people per square mile (1.8km) for Somerset and Dorset as a whole, and eight for Devon. Bristol, on the other hand, had a population density of about 40 people per square mile (1.8km), twice the size of the average *Domesday* settlement population density of 20 people. Moreover Bristol, although only a fifth of the size of Keynsham in area, was paying a comparable amount of tax, indicating that the manor had another, alternative source of income other than agriculture; and it was sufficiently prosperous to encourage the lords of other settlements to build properties there. Thus, while showing the continued value of agriculture to the City's prosperity, the *Domesday Book* also bears tacit witness to the rising importance of trade on Bristol's fortunes, an importance which would increase in the century after the Norman Conquest.

# 7  Anglo-Saxon costume and household goods

Despite the finds of loom weights and spindle whorls, no remains of any Saxon or Viking looms have been found in Bristol. This, unfortunately, is very much in keeping with the European picture in general, forcing modern archaeologists to base their reconstructions of early medieval looms on the traditional types still used in Scandinavian folk culture. The close positioning of two post holes in one of the buildings in Bristol suggests that they were dug to hold the posts of an upright loom, as were certain trenches dug below ground level along some of the buildings' walls, again possibly to hold an upright loom securely and bring it, perhaps, down to the weaver's height.

Unfortunately, most of the domestic items of eleventh-century Bristolians have perished with their owners. The smallest houses do not even seem to have been fitted with benches, and the commonest items found within buildings tend to be only hearths and loom weights. This suggests they were probably work-shops rather than homes. From this it might be concluded that the commonest industrial buildings were weaving sheds, of which the timber building in St Mary le Port Street was one. The lack of any furniture found in Bristol therefore seems to support the view that the buildings were primarily industrial.

Despite this, a number of smaller items have been found in Bristol during archaeological excavations, which give a brief glimpse into the kind of things Bristolians wore and used during the foundation of their city before the Conquest. Apart from the pottery and coinage mentioned earlier in this book, a small number of objects were recovered from St Mary le Port Street and Bristol Castle. From the Castle comes a square-shanked object with a flat end, shaped by hand and believed to be a scoop for ointment; a flat finger-ring of the penannular type, and a fragment of another ring, of half round section which expands towards the broken end. All were forged from copper.

Iron objects recovered include a pin with a spiral at one end (perhaps used for retaining a latch), a single-edged knife, and the broken remains of a padlock key. This is quite an interesting find, as both the Vikings and English used keys and padlocks which were developed from Roman locks. Part of the adornment of pagan Anglo-Saxon women had been chatelains or girdle-hangers, items of jewellery which hung from their belts, as the name suggests. Many of these objects are now thought to represent keys, symbolising their wearers' mastery over the household goods.

Apart from spindle whorls and the fragments of the forge stone, the only other stone object recovered from the Castle site dating from the Anglo-Saxon period was a whetstone. This in itself is quite important. A number of whetstones were found at St Mary le Port Street, a mixed collection of Pennant Sandstone, Wackes and Norwegian Ragstone. The Castle whetstone is a Coal Measures Sandstone, probably pennant grit. It contains particles of feldspar, angular quartz, muscovite sericite and iron rust, possibly from the knives and other objects it was used to sharpen. The pores in the stone had been filled using a black, opaque substance. Hones were a necessity of Anglo-Saxon daily life. Tools and knives had to be kept sharp, and were not easily replaced. Iron to the British peoples of the eleventh century was as valuable as silver is today. Hones were pierced at one end, and men of the period wore them around their necks as they went with their work. Later in the Middle Ages large amounts of Norwegian Ragstone was imported for these hones, and the finds in Bristol clearly point to Bristol's enduring contact with the Scandinavian world. Also found amongst the twelfth-century levels was a hammerstone of red sandstone, possibly dating from before the medieval period.

From St Mary le Port Street comes a variety of similar small finds. A Viking -style pin, and possible parts of a set of Viking scales, both made of copper alloy, were also found at the site. From the church itself came shroud pins, which were possibly pre-Conquest in date. Small though these finds are, they provide stout evidence of the industrial activities being carried out in Bristol at this time, with the scales (if they are such) in particular providing eloquent testimony to the city's mercantile status. The rings and pins also show that Bristolians were not unconcerned with their personal adornment, and so presumably kept up with the latest fashions.

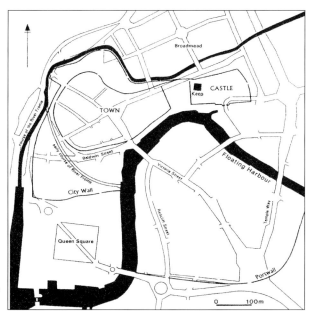

**24** *Location of the Castle Keep and the town walls.* Courtesy of Les Good

**25** *Remains of Bristol Castle Keep looking towards Broad Weir*

In addition to these have been the very rare finds of two strap-ends from the area around Bristol. One was found at Blaise Castle in 1813, while another was given to the City museum in 1986 after being found in an open field near Court Farm in Winterbourne. Strap-ends were tongue-like strips of metal used to decorate the ends of belts. The Winterbourne piece is 2.2in (5.6cm) long, showing a stylized human figure with one arm raised to touch its 'splayed-out' hair, while the legs curve round to form a complex inter-laced motif, one limb doubling back diagonally to end in a bulge around the human figure's stomach, possibly representing a serpent. Although it has been claimed to be in the Winchester style, the human figure is a marked departure from the animal and plant figures conventionally used, and lacks the style's symmetry. There is a parallel, though, with another hair-pulling figure, number T-25, found in the *Gloucester Tables* set, which may indicate that this is a Romanesque motif, though one that is still poorly understood. The *Gloucester Tables* set was excavated in 1983 from a rubbish pit of the first castle erected in 1068 in Gloucester. Fragments of early Medieval Ware pottery found with the tables suggest that the rubbish pit was dug no later than 1120, and possibly within the eleventh century. Assuming the similar-ities are not coincidental, this may indicate that the Winterbourne strap-end is of similar late, Saxo-Norman date. Regardless of the precise date of the ornament, it is a superb object, made all the more fascinating and valuable because of the lack of similar finds from the area.

# 8 The impact of the Normans

The Norman invasion of 1066 brought the Saxon era to an end. Thereafter, the court and aristocracy became French-speaking, and more closely concerned with events in Normandy and France. England's political ties moved south from Scandinavia to the warmer climes of western France. Throughout England the Saxon nobility were dispossessed in favour of Norman potentates. By 1086 only two of the Anglo-Scandinavian lords, Thurkill of Arden and Colswein of Lincoln, still held land directly of the king. These men fared better than the last two surviving earls: Gospatric was deprived of the earldom of Northumbria in 1072, and became an outlaw on the Scots borders, while his successor, Waltheof, was executed as a traitor after giving his support to the rebellion of Roger, earl of Hereford.

The situation in Gloucestershire followed events everywhere else. Under Edward the Confessor there had been 180 secular landlords in the county; under William this number dropped to 56, of whom only nine minor lords were English. The greatest Saxon magnate in the shire was Brictric FitzAlgar, who held 44,000 acres (17,813ha) within it. Although in the first three years after the Conquest he was left free to enjoy his lands, retaining his post as Sheriff, by 1086 it had all been confiscated, with the exception of his estates in Leckhampton and Woodchester. Many of the English rebels against William in the early part of his reign were undoubtedly selfish adventurers seeking their chance now that the bonds of society had weakened. The question remains, however, of how many had been forced into rebellion after the confiscation of their patrimonies.

A similar dispossession of native clerics occurred in the church. By 1087 the only remaining bishops consecrated before the Conquest had sees in and around Bristol. These two were Giso, Bishop of Wells, which then covered much of what is now Somerset, and Wulfstan of Worcester, who held 5 hides in Westbury on Trym. Soon these two passed away, to be succeeded by French clergy of the Conquerors' appointment. Wells was given to John de Villula, one of the Conqueror's doctors and a native of Tours, who moved its seat to Bath. Worcester came under the sway of Samson, brother of the Archbishop of York. The major monasteries and abbeys were similarly affected, so that only the smallest still retained English abbots. This probably little affected the parish priests, who occupied far too low a position to be of much concern to the Norman overlords. Despite the drives against clerical marriage initiated by the Conqueror and his new Archbishop of Canterbury, Lanfranc, the parish clergy still took wives. Their economic position followed the same development as the *villeins'*, becoming depressed after an initial period of little change.

In Bristol this cataclysm was marked by the eviction of a number of citizens by Geoffrey of Coutances to build his castle. As a royal manor, Bristol and Barton Regis had quickly passed into the hands of England's new king, who gave the land to the bishop of Coutances. He had earlier acquired 112 acres (45.34ha) of meadow in Bedminster to guard the Avon. By 1086 his lands stretched from there to Westbury on Trym and Henbury, including Harry Stoke and Hambrook. The most obvious symbol of his power was this fortress. At first only a motte and bailey fort, it expanded into a solid stone stronghold that resisted attack until it became 'one of those ruins that Cromwell knocked about a bit'.

The Normans built castles everywhere, symbols of their dominance and the new order. By 1100 5,000–6,000 of them had been built throughout the country. Bishop Geoffrey was not the only Norman landowner in the Bristol area though. Arnulf of Hesdin received Hanham, while Thornbury, one of the manors of Britric FitzAlgar, became property of Matilda, William's queen, who rented it to one Hunfrid. After her death in 1088 her son, William Rufus, gave it to Robert FitzHamon for his help in putting down Odo's rebellion in the same year.

This was not the only estate near Bristol that FitzHamon had acquired. In 1087 Rufus gave it to him as part of the honour of Gloucester. It had previously been the property of Edward the Confessor's queen Edith, the sister of Earl Harold, as part of the manor of Keynsham. After the Conquest, Edith retained it until her death in 1075, when it escheated to the crown. Much of the Bristol area was held by the church, and so when the abbeys passed into the hands of Norman clerics, so did it. St Mary's of Worcester continued to hold Westbury on Trym, Henbury, Redwick and Stoke Bishop, and through the manor's possession, two houses in Bristol. Pucklechurch was the property of St Mary's at Glastonbury, whose prior was the notoriously violent Turstin of Caen. Osbern, one of the Conqueror's closest friends, who became Bishop of Exeter, was given Oldland.

The great lords let the land to their vassals. From the Bishop of Coutances Herlwin and Azelin both held parts of Bishopsworth. Knowle and Bedminster remained royal land, Knowle being let out to Osborne Giffard, while Bedminster remained within the king's demesne. A few Anglo-Saxon landowners do appear, though. Thurstan, son of Rolf, held 5 hides in Aust. Oswulf held Hambrook from Bishop Geoffrey, Dunn, one of the few pre-Conquest landowners, held Bitton, and one Hunbald had Hanham. Hunfrid's name suggests that he, too, was English. The events of 1066 were traumatic, yet Bristol survived, and trade carried on much as before.

One effect of this was that not only did some holdings of the Saxon nobility survive the Norman Conquest, but they later became knights' fees, although there has as yet been no convincing argument definitively equating the decimally based quotas of the Norman period with the decimally arranged hides, or the duo-decimally arranged *carucates* of the Anglo-Scandinavian kingdom. One such survival may be the estates of the six *radcnihts* recorded at Henbury by the *Domesday Book*. Although by the time of Henry II only one *radcniht*, Ainulf or Einulf, is recorded as holding 0.5 hides of land at Charlton in Henbury, the fees held by Richard de Coveley of 1.5 hides in Wick in Redland, 2 hides in Redland by Roger de Vehm, a single hide by Richard de Vehm, also in Redland, 2 hides by Walter de la Hay, and a single hide by Robert de Saltmarsh in Henbury, combined with Einulf's holding, are exactly equivalent to the 8 hides held by the six *radcnihts* of 1086, and it is quite possible that the six holdings together represent the actual holdings of the six *radcnihts* of the *Domesday Book*.

Some of them may even have been the descendants of the original riding men. Despite William's dispossession of the native English aristocracy, and decree that no English monk or clergyman should be promoted to any position of honour in the church, by the accession of Henry II some English families were once again rising to prominence. This was assisted by sections of the Norman aristocracy attempting to bolster their claims to their lands by marrying into the old Saxon nobility, just as Henry I had done with Matilda, the daughter of Malcolm III of Scotland. Thus Gervase FitzRoger, a Norman baron, some time before 1136 married Agnes, the daughter of Edward of Cornhill, a member of the London *Cnihtengild*, also taking his father-in-law's English name. The name 'Lewin's Mead', if indeed a form of Leofwine, would testify to the continued importance around Bristol of native English magnates, particularly if the Lewin after whom the meadow was named was the son of Aelfric.

A similar process may have been at work in Bristol to promote the FitzHarding family. The founder of the dynasty, Harding, was the king's reeve in Bristol, living in a modest residence in Baldwin Street. He was evidently a skilled lawyer, for William of Malmesbury describes him as fighting with forensic rather than military skill. His name, Harding, suggests he was English, rather than Norman, or at least, like Gervase FitzRoger, that he had English relations. His son, Robert FitzHarding, lived in the same house after his father's death around 1115, until he built 'a great stone house by the Frome', possibly the same stone house excavated at Tower Hill in 1982. Ambitious and acquisitive, FitzHarding augmented his modest inheritance by purchasing the manor of Billeswick and Bedminster. At Billeswick he founded the Augustinian abbey, which was to become Bristol Cathedral after the reformation. His wife, Eva, shared her husband's religious patronage, and in 1190 founded another Augustinian house, this time for canonesses, near the top of St Michael's Hill, endowing it with lands in Southmead for its support.

FitzHarding, like his overlord, the Earl of Gloucester, was a staunch supporter of the Angevin cause during Stephen's reign. Indeed, the future Henry II had lodged in the City as a boy and was probably personally acquainted with FitzHarding. As a result, after the Angevin victory the FitzHarding family were rewarded with the confiscated lands of Roger of Berkeley, until FitzHarding's estates in Gloucester and Somerset included Redcliffe, Bedminster, Hartcliffe, Abbot's Leigh, Tickenham, Portbury, Portishead, Horfield, Weston, Farmborough, Baggridge, Weacombe, Sandford, Pawlett, Almondsbury, Elberton, Ashworthy, Hill, Cromhall, Wotton under Edge, Ozleworth, Beverston, Newington Bagpath, Kingscote, Uley, Dursley, Cam, Alkington, Sharpness, Hurst, Hinton, Slimbridge, Coaley, Nympsfield, Clingre, Gossington, Arlingham and, of course, Berkeley, as well as more in Devon, Dorset, Wiltshire, and Warwickshire.

Included in Berkeley hundred was the *tithing* of Filton, representatives of which were required to attend the yearly Leet Court at Berkeley at least until 1618. Indeed, it was only at the re-organization of local government in the nineteenth century that Filton ceased to be part of the hundred. Classed as part of Horfield in the *Domesday Book*, Filton possibly only became a separate parish in 1142 when Robert FitzHarding endowed St Augustine's Abbey in Bristol with 6 *messuages* of land in Filton, though administratively these *messuages* were still considered part of the manor of Horfield. Horfield itself had been one of the estates given to FitzHarding by Henry I. Like much of the Bristol area, the Crown had been a major landowner at the time of the *Domesday Book*, which records that the king held 8 hides of land there. Horfield Church itself may have been the pre-Conquest chapelry of Almondsbury. It was subsequently rebuilt by the Normans in the twelfth century.

The career of the FitzHarding dynasty illustrates the growing importance of the towns in Anglo-Norman politics, and the relative fluidity of the early twelfth-century social hierarchy, in which an enterprising and ambitious burgess could rise to the aristocracy, just as an enterprising Saxon merchant did in the century before the Conquest. The Bishop of Winchester could describe Londoners as baron-like in England because of the size of their city, and showed no surprise that they should claim to elect the king. FitzHarding's life expands this statement to cover Bristol: it was not just in the metropolis that rich citizens acted as and became barons.

Undoubtedly the greatest figure in local politics, however, was another Robert, the Earl of Gloucester, the eldest of the illegitimate sons of Henry I, who had been invested with the former lands of the Bishop of Coutances after they had been confiscated by the Crown on the rebellious bishop's death in 1093. Bristol had then been given to Robert FitzHamon, one of the few barons who had remained loyal to William Rufus. FitzHamon's sprawling territories included lands in Gloucester and Glamorgan, which he had won by conquest. At his death, Henry gave his heiress, Mabel, to Robert, creating him as earl of Gloucester. Bristol Castle became his principal residence, and probably the administrative centre of his earldom to such an extent that quite often twelfth-century chroniclers referred to him as the earl of Bristol rather than of Gloucester. The castle housed the earl's administrative staff of clerks who wrote his charters and other business documents, and there may even have been an exchequer after the royal model: there was certainly one in operation there between 1173-83, the last ten years of earl William's life. Robert dominated the Angevin cause to such an extent that the Anarchy was sometimes called 'the earl of Bristol's war', despite his claim that he only fought for Mars when he had to, but served Venus as a volunteer. A cultured patron of learning with a reputation for encouraging poetry and literature, it was he who engaged Adelard of Bath as tutor for the young Henry of Anjou when he stayed with him at Bristol. Adelard was one of the great figures of the twelfth-century renaissance, a popularizer of the new Moslem science now entering Christendom from Sicily and Spain. It was to the young Henry that he dedicated his *Libellus de Opere Astrolapsus*, or *Treatise on the Astrolabe*. Under Robert's aegis, Bristol became not only a rival centre to London politically, but also culturally.

Like FitzHarding, Robert was a patron of the new religious orders. It was he who founded the first Benedictine house in Bristol, a cell of his great abbey at Tewkesbury on the site of the present St James' Church. It was the earl of Gloucester, too, who granted the future Temple Fee to the new order of the Knights Templars, warrior monks of St Bernard founded in 1118 who, with their brothers the Hospitallers, became in Palestine the embodiment of the Church Militant.

Elsewhere in the Bristol area churches were being built or refounded. One of these was Westbury on Trym, which Wulfstan obtained from the Conqueror to rebuild as a daughter house of the see of Worcester around 1093. According to William of Malmesbury this was a comprehensive task, as the church was considerably dilapidated, half fallen down, and without half its roof, so that he had to rebuild it upwards from the foundations, repairing the walls with worked masonry, and placing new lead on the roof. The church's new endowment included a glebe house, tithes, and office books, with Wulfstan's biographer Coleman as its prior. Regrettably this new foundation did not last, and the monks were expelled by Abbot Sampson in favour of secular canons some time before the end of his abbacy in 1112. Bishop Simon of Worcester reversed this situation 13 years later by returning Westbury Church to the prior and monks of Worcester, along with its daughter chapels of St Wereburge on Henbury Hill and Compton.

After the Norman invasion not only was Bristol fortified, but it also played a vital role in the construction of other fortifications on the Welsh frontier. Chepstow Castle, Strigoil, guarding the River Wye, was deliberately sited by its founder, William FitzOsbern, on a natural harbour so that it could be supplied from Bristol all the year round. This was part of an emerging pattern of urban settlement and expansion during the next century. Water navigation formed a vital means of communication at a time when land travel could be difficult and lengthy. As the Middle Ages wore on, nearly half of all new towns were ports on estuaries or the coast exporting goods from their hinterlands.

**26** *Bristol Castle Keep from the north-west*

The majority of these were, like Bristol, in southern England. In Wales, 24 of these new towns were built on the coast, the majority established by the English, and like Strigoil supplied with provisions and personnel for their garrisons by ship from England.

Occupying such a strategically important location, and itself strongly fortified, it was inevitable that Bristol should become involved in the strife following the death of the Conqueror, as his sons Robert and William competed for the throne. In 1088 the Bishop of Coutances and his nephew, Robert de Mowbray, used Bristol as their base, whence they attacked Rufus' supporters in Bath and Wiltshire. During the Anarchy, Bristol became Robert's base of operations for the Angevin cause, again directing his attacks against Bath. In June 1138 Geoffrey de Talbot, one of Stephen's supporters, deserted him for Earl Robert, but was later caught reconnoitering Bath with two other knights. Talbot's captivity did not last long, however; the Bristolian garrison, led by Earl William, marched against Bishop Robert who led the forces from Bath, and informed him that unless he released Talbot they would hang him and his companions. With this terrible incentive before him, the bishop gave in, much to the wrath of Stephen.

This incident provoked a response. Stephen himself sent a large army to Bath and marched on Bristol, which had become notorious to the chroniclers of the time through the tortures invented by one of the earl's relatives, Philip Gay, whose cruelty was compared to that of Nero and Decius. Advised by his followers to build two motte and bailey siege castles either side of the town to force its surrender, Stephen besieged Bristol, but despite plots to fill in the river with turfs and stone, the castle held out. Stephen raised the siege to assault the earl's other fortresses of Castle Cary and Harptree in Somerset.

In 1139 the anarchy entered a new phase when another of her supporters, William d'Aubigny dispatched ambassadors to Matilda at Anjou, inviting her to come to England. Landing with Matilda at Arundel, the earl left to raise troops in Wallingford and Bristol. He was disappointed. On his return to the south coast he found that Stephen had marched on the town, forcing its chatelaine, Queen Adeliza, to hand over Matilda. The surrender had not been unconditional, however. Adeliza released Matilda only on the condition that she would be given safe passage to Bristol, an agreement which Stephen, often close to treachery himself, surprisingly honoured.

It was not long before Stephen himself joined her as her prisoner. Captured on 2 February 1141 at Lincoln while battling the earl's forces, Stephen was taken to Bristol where he first enjoyed some freedom of movement before being placed in chains at the instigation of Matilda herself, an act which, along with the Empress' notoriously haughty personality, further alienated her supporters. Stephen was not there long. Earl Robert was himself captured attacking Winchester, and released by the king's supporters in exchange for Stephen. The City continued to play a vital strategic role in the conflict, however, with Matilda's son, the future Henry II entering the city in 1147 from Dursley, and again in 1153 on another tour through England.

The city itself continued to expand. Although outside the Saxon town walls, the area immediately to the east of the Castle on the main road to London emerged as the *Feria*, which three centuries later had become known as Old Market. *Feria* can mean both 'fair' and 'market', and although the latter were certainly known in Anglo-Saxon England, fairs were largely introduced by the Normans. The only explicit pre-Conquest reference to a fair in England is the grant of a *gearmarkett* in a charter of 1053-5 to Stow St Mary in Lincolnshire. By 1150 there are records of a *burgage* tenement and houses in the *Feria*, suggesting it was consciously founded as a trading suburb, probably as an open market with space for booths and stalls similar to the other wide market streets founded elsewhere in the same period, and likewise enjoying the grant of certain borough privileges. The establishment of Old Market moved the centre of trade from the west to the eastern end of the city. Early references to St Mary le Port as St Mary *in Foro*, St Mary in the Market, suggests that before the foundation of Old Market the main trading area was located there.

Yet another district, the *novum burgum de prato*, 'new borough of the meadow', or, as it is now, Broadmead, was founded either by Earl Robert himself or his son William between the new Benedictine priory of St James and the Castle, with the priory church serving as its parish church. This too was granted a market, which began to attract traders from elsewhere in England. Robert or his son was also responsible for the foundation of St Michael's church on the hill north-west of the town overlooking Frome Gate, though its earliest mention is in a charter of 1174. Additionally, Robert had been responsible for rebuilding Bristol Castle, and its earliest remains are substantially his. He may also have been largely responsible for building the town's Norman defences. If so, then the topography of early medieval Bristol surely bears the stamp of his powerful and dominating personality.

South of the river, Redcliffe began to be occupied during the first half of the twelfth century, as the flat open land between the Bridge and Redcliffe Hill offered more space than was available in the walled borough, while the anchorage was deeper on that side due to the river's natural currents, and offered a better site for the construction of quays. The suburb prospered so that by 1210 it was given the same tax assessment as Bristol itself, while the church of St Mary Redcliffe was already in existence by 1158, when it was confirmed as a property of Sarum cathedral. Again, it may well have had its origins in a pre-Conquest chapel, in this case one of St John's in Bedminster.

In architecture, much of the Saxon tradition was preserved. It is often difficult to distinguish whether eleventh-century churches were built before or after the Conquest, as English Romanesque architecture remained largely unchanged. It is after the Normans in the twelfth century, however, that the first secular stone houses seem to have been built, though even then they were still sufficiently rare as to cause remark. The stone used tends to be the locally available materials, such as that taken from the quarries on Dundry, Durdham Downs and Brislington, rather than the Caen stone imported elsewhere in the country (for example at Winchester), though Caen stone does seem to have been used in the Castle keep. The use of stone, even local varieties, was a sign of wealth. The stone quays built at Dundas Wharf in the second quarter of the twelfth century may have been local Pennant Sandstone, but they rank as some of the first in the country. Stone does not appear on the waterfront in London until later in the twelfth century, and it was only in the fourteenth and fifteenth centuries that it became common elsewhere. In constructing these quays Bristolians were making a solid, concrete statement of the City's wealth. Seaborne trade, embodied in the new stone docks, were the very foundation of the City's wealth.

There was no immediate change in pottery either. The locally produced Saxon wares remained popular alongside foreign and domestic imports well after the Conquest. The forms of these wares do change, however, though except in specific cases foreign influence or origin is not obvious. Most of the new designs were probably the result of a development of previous insular traditions, rather than innovations following a foreign model. It is only from the mid-thirteenth century that new, intrusive imports, often French, become obvious.

Even urbanisation itself came out of Anglo-Saxon traditions. The *burhs*, which served to guard England against the Vikings, acted as trading posts as well as garrisons, and their population may have been augmented by refugees fleeing the Norse invaders. The Normans, however, were determined to hang on to what they had gained, and even to expand it if possible. Everywhere the

Normans settled, profitable towns from London to Dublin were enlarged, rebuilt and modernised. Bristol was one of those cities.

One new trade appears in Bristol in the later twelfth century. The chronicler Richard of Devizes, writing with his characteristic bile, reported that there was no one in Bristol who either was not, or had not been, a soapmaker. Well, at least the burgesses were clean. Having said that, Bristol got off better than most of the other cities in England. Richard hated Bath because it was surrounded by vaporous marshland as though it were actually at the mouth of Hell; Chester and York were too close to violent and dangerous Welshmen and Scots (respectively); and London was a sink of iniquity and sexual vice. There did not seem to be too many places he did like.

Bristol was rapidly becoming a prosperous port. From its obscure beginnings it had become a rival, both in size, wealth and military power, to the far more ancient city of Bath. Writing some time in the 1130s, the anonymous writer of the *Gesta Stephani* went somewhat further, describing Bristol as 'the richest city almost of all the cities of this country, receiving merchandize from neighbouring and foreign places . . . by situation the most defensible of any city in England . . . a most safe and convenient port for a thousand ships.' It was an exaggeration, but not by much. Although it only became the second most important port in England during the reign of Henry VIII, after the middle of the twelfth century it was considered by many to be the third most powerful city in England. Yet, although then small and of little significance, it was in the Anglo-Saxon period that the foundations of its greatness were firmly laid.

# 9 The City's defences: castle and town walls

While the original Saxon fortifications may have consisted of nothing more substantial than a defensive ditch and timber palisade, this was replaced by Geoffrey of Coutances under the Normans with a more substantial stone structure, and with a second, outer wall traditionally considered to have been constructed later in the first half of the twelfth century, possibly by Robert of Gloucester, though it may also date from the thirteenth century, possibly contemporary with the later Marsh wall. This second wall enclosed the area bounded by the Frome immediately to the north of the town. It ran from New Gate to Frome Gate, whence it turned to join St John's Gate almost immediately south-east of it along the present Christmas Street. This was the first of the two further projects to enclose the expanding town in defensive walling, the last being the enclosure of the suburbs of the Marsh, Redcliffe and Temple Fee *c.*1240, during the diversion of the Frome.

These building projects made Bristol, with Lincoln, Norwich and York, the only cities in medieval England to develop the system of concentric rings of defensive walls found in continental cities. Remains of the early Norman town wall dated to the first half of the twelfth century have been found at Peter Street, stretching along Tower Lane from the Upper Pithay Gate to the former St John's Arch, or the Blind Arch, a section of medieval wall demolished in 1911 at the end of John Street. This stretch of wall was interpreted in the original excavation of 1901 to be the foundation of Bristol's inner wall, about 6ft (1.82m) wide and 370ft (112.77m) long in total, and not exceeding 8ft (2.438cm) in height, though the original height of the wall above ground could not be established. A short distance from St John's churchyard along the wall stood the remains of the eponymous Tower, 23.5ft (7.16m) in diameter, which was still standing in 1821 as part of a house when the antiquarian Samuel Seyer wrote his *Memoirs of Bristol*. Previous development had disturbed the wall's remains, so that it did not come to a definite, planned end at the Upper Pithay Gateway, but a ditch was discovered below the wall at this location, with the land sloping away towards the Frome, though it is unknown whether this formed part of the defences.

Excavations along the south side of Newgate, almost at the junction of Union Street, revealed an area of masonry breached at one point by a 1.5m gap, the remnants of a doorway. The buff mortar used in the masonry suggested that it might have been part of the twelfth-century city wall, possibly the south side of the twelfth-century Old Gate, which was demolished *c*.1305. The same yellow-brown sandy mortar is also found in the western curtain wall and the keep of Bristol Castle, suggesting that the Norman town walls, or at least what remains of them, were built by Robert of Gloucester rather than Geoffrey of Coutances.

The psychological effect of the walls' construction was to prove particularly enduring, lasting far longer indeed than most of the medieval city walls themselves. By encircling the town, the walls came to embody a rigid and enduring definition of its physical limits, perhaps creating a sense of snobbishness and superiority, even when urban sprawl had rendered the definition out-moded and obsolete. To older generations of citizens, true Bristolians were those born within the walls. Those who had the misfortune to be born 'outside the gates', even if they came from a genteel background in one of the nearby areas, such as Bedminster, were nevertheless considered somehow lacking in their background. This parochialism survived until the Second World War and the post-war building boom, which radically changed the City's geography on the one hand, while the new post-war prosperity and geographical mobility further undermined local differences as people moved more easily not only from one side of the City, but from one part of the country to another.

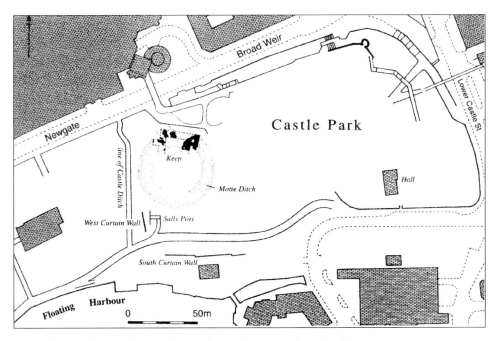

**27**  *Castle Park, showing location of keep and motte.* Courtesy of Les Good

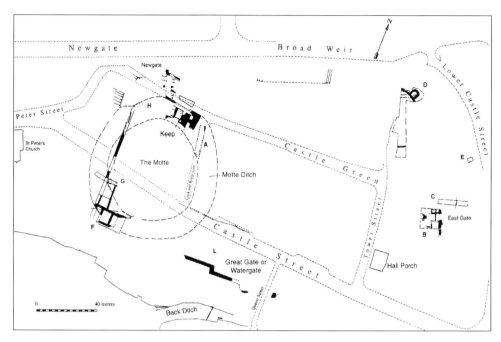

**28** *Bristol Castle: Plan of excavated sites 1948-70, showing keep and motte.* Courtesy of Les Good

The Norman's first important feat of military engineering in Bristol, however, was the Castle. Although Coutance's receipt of a third of the City's taxes suggests that he was then constable of the Castle, or enjoying a similar post, there is no reference to a Castle in Bristol itself until 1088, when the *Anglo-Saxon Chronicle* records the bishop and his nephew sallying forth from the Castle to ravage Bath and the surrounding countryside, and so laying waste the district of Berkeley Harness. Its siting within the *burh* defences, however, would nevertheless argue for an earlier date, as the earliest castles were not the later Norman *mottes*, but enclosures built against earlier fortifications, such as in London where the Norman Castle was constructed up against the Roman and Saxon defences. The explanation for this silence in the *Domesday Book* may lie in the relatively small part of the borough destroyed to make way for the Castle's construction. Although the Castle was built within and utilising the defences of the original Saxon *burh*, with houses demolished to make room for it (as at Exeter, Chepstow, York, Lincoln and Northampton), no tenements in the main area of settlement were destroyed. In its earliest stage the Castle may have been a simple ringwork, as suggested by a deeply-cut ditch found at the north-east corner and east gate of the Castle, though no evidence for it has come from the south side and south-west corner. Ringworks were relatively simple castles in which the lord's dwelling was enclosed within an embankment capped by a wooden stockade, and further encircled with a defensive ditch. The entrance, approached by a narrow wooden bridge, was sometimes protected by a wooden tower. Additionally, the Bishop of Coutances is believed to have strengthened the timber fortifications with stone defences linking the Castle to the main borough.

Some time later, possibly around 1080, the ringwork Castle was redeveloped into a *motte* and bailey fortress. This style consisted of a courtyard, the bailey, surrounded by an embankment topped by a wooden palisade. This embankment was, in turn, surrounded by a defensive ditch. Within the bailey was the *motte*, a defensive mound and the strongest part of the fortress, defended yet again by a second ditch and surmounted by another wooden stockade and watchtower. The *motte* at Bristol Castle was located just east of Peter Street, with the modern Castle Street running just south of its centre. Just over 61m in diameter, its eastern side passed a little beyond the former Cock and Bottle Lane. This was surrounded by a ditch with an external diameter of 83m, 12m wide in some parts and over 6m deep, narrowing to a flat bottom. This was probably due to frequent cleaning, the small holes found inside it being steps to facilitate the entry of workmen to perform this unpleasant task, or perhaps hold poles for scaffolding.

Just beyond the *motte* ditch on the later north wall of the Castle Keep was a V-shaped ditch, considered by archaeologists to be part of the original bailey ditch. This was approximately 5m wide, but widened by another 2m shortly before meeting the *motte* ditch. Possibly contemporary with the *motte* was a cross wall running across the *motte* ditch around 3.5m from the east wall of the later keep. It was 1.35-1.40m at its top, built over some 9.8-11.8in (25-30cm) of infill in the ditch. It is probable that the wall is all that is left of a circular curtain wall flanking the *motte*, possibly built just after the *motte* ditch had

**29** *The Castle curtain wall and defences from the west*

become partially silted, so allowing the wall to be built atop the infill material rather than directly upwards from the bottom of the ditch, as would be expected if the wall was exactly contemporary with the building of the *motte*.

Thirty or fourty years after the construction of this early fortress, Robert of Gloucester began the building of the stone keep which was to turn Bristol Castle into one of the strongest fortresses in England. Two manuscript calendars state that work began on the keep in 1110, a date supported by the lack of Ham Green Ware pottery in the Castle refuse, which suggests that the keep was built no later than 1120. On the other hand, the gift of building stone from Robert's foundation of St James' Priory would suggest a far later date of 1137-47, though this in turn seems unlikely considering that the turbulent conditions of the Anarchy would allow little time for elaborate building work. It may be, however, that like the *motte* and its curtain wall, although the keep itself was substantially built before Henry's death in 1135, work was still being done elsewhere in the structure.

The north-east corner of Robert's keep was built on top of the original *motte* and bailey ditches, the east side of the latter being cut back and stepped on its east side to support the keep's foundations. South of the keep's west face the remains of an adjoining building were found, integral to the keep. The walls of this additional structure proceeded slightly to the north. Abutting the Cross Wall on its east side, north of the *motte* ditch was a stepped revetment

**30** *The south-eastern remnants of the Castle Keep*

**31** *Crenellations old and new: Bristol Castle Keep and the modern entrance to Castle Park at Newgate*

of pennant sandstone which, however, underlay the Cross Wall on the opposite side. West of the Cross Wall the revetment only existed on the top of the ditch slope, although 31.5in (80cm) beyond there was a similar structure built on top of the ditch silt, projecting like a buttress against the wall of the keep, which itself overlay the stonework of the revetment.

Apart from the foundation of the keep itself, whose floor was 8ft (243.8m) thick, three wells were found running towards the river, about 80ft (24.38m) apart. One of these was 6 or 10ft (1.83/3.04m) in diameter, and 38-40ft (11.58-12.19m) deep. Amongst the material filling this well were fragments of Caen stone, supporting the traditional view that Robert partly used this material for the Castle. Horrifically, this well also contained the skeleton of an adolescent, perhaps 10 to 15 years old, and the arm bones of another adult skeleton. It is unknown, though sadly not unimaginable, what tragedy or atrocity led to the well as their last resting place. Perhaps they had been the unfortunate recipients of the tender attention of Philip Gay.

Near the middle of this 'main block' of the keep's north-east foundations was a latrine or rubbish pit, 2.9m long by 1.8m wide and extending 2.75m below the level of the surviving wall. This sloped up in its north-east corner to form a stone-lined *garderobe* chute 15.7in (40cm) wide. In addition to this refuse chute, there was a section 21.6in (55cm) from the expected north corner of the shaft where the wall turned to the north, suggesting another such chute, with a similar feature found on the shaft's south sides. Another *garderobe* was found on the inside of the keep's north-west corner. Amongst the coprolites recovered from the *garderobe* chute were recovered fruit stones, and small animal bones suggesting the rich diet of the Castle's personnel.

The northern edge of the keep's foundations crossed the *motte* ditch, which was 20-25ft (6.09-7.62m) wide at the top, and extended 12.5ft

(3.81m) below the level of the cellar. The remains of the western end of the keep's northern wall where it entered the bailey ditch were approximately 5m thick. At the same time as the keep was being built, the *motte* ditch was deliberately filled in, with soil dumped against the sides of the keep where they built directly into the ditch. The ditch under the keep was kept open until the fourteenth century, however, either as a *garderobe* or a dungeon, though this is perhaps unlikely as a castle of Bristol's stature would have had separate prisons in the bailey area, towers in the curtain walls and secure rooms within the keep itself. The foundations of the keep were almost entirely of pennant sandstone, quarried from Kingswood, which Robert probably held in wardship on behalf of his father, Henry I, and fragments of oolitic limestone from Dundry.

Despite the excavation of the keep, there are still two questions that remain unanswered: the actual dimensions of the keep itself, and the number of towers it possessed. William Worcester in his *Itinerary* gives two sets of dimensions for the tower, one his own measurements and the second that of the Castle porter. The porter's measurements are 60ft (18.28m) from east to west, and 45ft (13.71m) from north to south. Worcester himself gives the length of the east side as 108ft (32.91m), and the length of the west and south sides as 90ft (2743m) each. Not only do these measurements conflict with each other, they also conflict with the lengths of the surviving walls excavated in 1989. Seyer in the nineteenth century considered the porter's measurements to be internal. When the thickness of the castle walls themselves – 25ft (7.62m) according to the porter – was added, the size of the

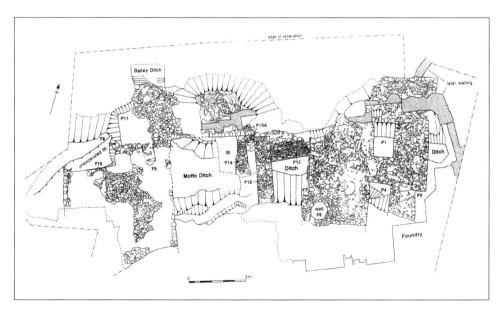

**32** *Remains of motte and bailey ditches, Bristol Castle Keep.* Courtesy of Les Good

**33** *North eastern walling of Bristol Castle keep*

keep from east to west becomes 110ft (33.53m), and 95ft (28.95m) from
north to south. The length of the north wall from east to west, however,
appears to have been 41ft (12.49m) internally, and 95 or 110ft (28.95 or
33.52m) externally. The difference in measurement between those of the
foundations and as given by Worcester could possibly be due to the latter
being made at a different level, such as that of the entrance, which may not
be directly aligned with the base of the wall. The north-west corner of the
keep, not found during the investigation in 1989, may actually be the west
face built on the sloping side of the bailey ditch, though it is possible that
this could really be an internal feature similar to those found in the north-
west corner. If the supposed extension of the west wall is considered as the
face of the keep's outer wall, and the north-west corner lined up with this,
then the north wall could be as long as 110ft (33.52m), or 95ft (28.95m) if
this extension is ignored. The difference in lengths between the east and
west sides may be due to the presence of a forebuilding, or, less likely, the
largest of the Castle's towers at the north-east or south-east corner, though
this was possibly separate from four other towers. It is also possible that
Worcester confused his directions when measuring the keep himself, and
that the longest side was the north rather than the east. This explanation
may not be necessary if it is accepted that Worcester's measurements were
approximate. He made them by physically pacing them out, rather than
using the more accurate techniques available to modern surveyors. Thus, the
north side may indeed be only 95ft (28.95m) long. On the other hand, this
could very well be correct if the alternative position for the north-west
corner of the keep is true, which would make the length of the north wall
110ft (33.52m).

It is also unclear how many towers the keep had. Worcester states that it had four, and that there was one tower the 'myghtyest toure above all the iiii toures'. This turret was perhaps 6ft (1.83m) taller than the others. It is not clear from this description whether this tower was one of the four, or an additional fifth structure. Millerd's plan of Bristol, published 17 years after its demolition, shows the keep with four towers and a fifth lying behind and to the left as seen from the Avon. Seyer considered this to be that of St Martin's Chapel, though this now seems after Michael Ponsford's 1979 investigation to lie further south and in the outer ward of the castle, rather more distant than the illustration suggests. Seyer also illustrated his discussion of the Castle with reproductions of the common seal of the burgesses of Bristol, from the time of Edward I, which seems to show the south-east corner tower larger than the rest; and the second mayoral seal from 1359 which Seyer considered showed a firepan placed on top of one of the towers to turn it into a beacon, though it does not show any great difference from the other towers and may really represent another, fifth and higher tower attached to the keep.

There is also the related question of the positions of the keep entrance and that of the possible fifth tower. The most likely possibility is the existence of a forebuilding at the east side of the keep, as the outer face of the most easterly wall and a turn in the north wall indicate the corners of a tower on the north-east side. This in turn suggests that an external staircase may have run south

**34** *Millerd's plan of Bristol Castle.* Courtesy of Les Good

**35** *The Castle curtain wall from the east, looking towards St Peter's*

**36** *The remains of the thirteenth-century royal hall, now used by the Parks Department*

along the eastern wall to an entrance on an upper storey. This would be typical of many private stone keeps, whose massive walls, protected by corner turrets, rose three or four stories high with a main entrance at first floor level approached by stairs and protected by a forebuilding.

There is also some ambiguity about the faced stonework in the north-west corner of the keep. If it is an internal feature, similar to that on the east side, it likewise suggests that the forebuilding and entrance were on the west side. This may hold true even if they are the remains of an external feature. It may, however, be the remains of a fifth tower, and that the apparent distance away from the Castle in Millerd's drawing is in fact a mistake. South of the *motte* were found the later remains of the west curtain wall, about 15m from the *motte's* western edge, and the south curtain wall situated a further 20m beyond that, and 15m to its east.

This new stone keep transformed Bristol Castle into one of the strongest and most impressive fortresses in England. *Motte* and bailey castles persisted in England until the thirteenth century, with only a few, the very strongest, constructed of stone. The stone keep at Bristol made the Castle the coun-

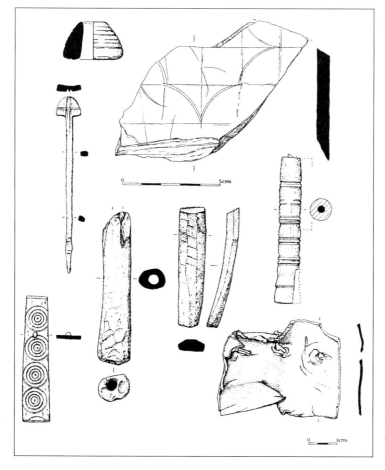

**37** *Norman bone, wood and pottery objects found at the keep.* Courtesy of Les Good

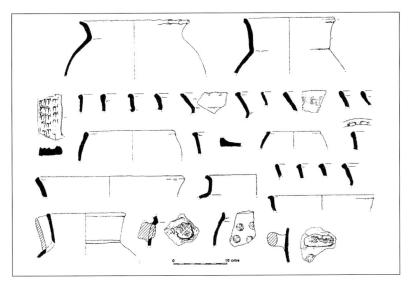

**38** *Norman pottery from Bristol Castle Keep.* Courtesy of Les Good

terpart of London, a stronghold still proud enough in the late thirteenth century to be described by the rhyming chronicler Robert of Gloucester as 'a castle with the noblest of towers; that, of all the keeps of England, is held the flower'. Bristol Castle was exceptionally impressive considering its lack of stone rivals nearby in the West Midlands. *Motte* and bailey castles were extensively used by the Normans along the marcher regions of Herefordshire and Shropshire, and the areas of Norman expansion into South Wales. Although simple and effective, the elaborate stone defences of the keep at Bristol would truly have made it stand out as a '*castrum fortissimum*', in the words of Simeon of Durham.

Although historical and archaeological research necessarily concentrates on the type of features common to castles in order to form a chronology and typology of their construction, the castle architects were uninterested in categories developed by modern historians; indeed, they would probably have not even recognised them. Medieval castles, even relatively simple forms such as the *motte* and bailey, show an endless variety in pattern and scale, suggesting that the medieval designers and their observers were more interested in their individuality than adherence to a particular type. Bristol Castle may similarly be a unique fortress, constructed according to the accepted principles of castle construction, but nevertheless retaining features individual to itself. Nevertheless, Bristol Castle shows a strong similarity to the keeps of Cary, Kenilworth, Middleham, Newcastle upon Tyne, Rising, Rochester and Walden castles, and a more distant kinship to that of Dover. It is even possible that the internal features of the castle now lost may have included ornamented windows and fireplaces, and arcades such as those boasted by Dover, Rochester and Hedingham.

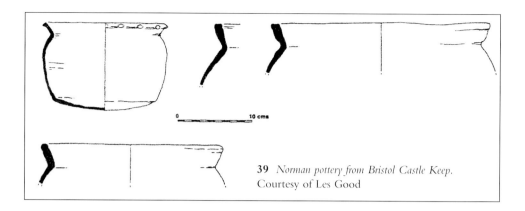

**39** *Norman pottery from Bristol Castle Keep.* Courtesy of Les Good

One piece of internal architecture which did manage to survive up to the Second World War was a Norman arch with a corridor area. Some of the internal mouldings from the Castle were later incorporated into one of the buildings built using the remains of the royal hall on the eastern edge of he Castle site. Although the present vaulted hall dates from later in the Middle Ages, it was built on top of a twelfth-century predecessor. Externally, the moat has survived as a major landscape feature at Castle Park to the present day, and its junction with the river and former course underneath Queen Street are also still visible.

A castle as strongly fortified as Bristol on a major port could not fail to attract royal attention. Although Robert was able to pass it on to his heir, Earl William, it was taken over by King John after William died in 1173, no doubt fearing that the Castle could recapitulate its role in Stephen's reign in the new rebellion breaking out against him. From the fourteenth century onwards the Castle was gradually allowed to fall into decay. It was already a ruin before the end of the fifteenth century, and parliament completed its destruction in 1659 by ordering its demolition. The site was then leased out by the corporation for development into tenements. Nevertheless, when walking round the remains of the 1989 archaeological investigations, laid out into a park, Bristolians can look back to a time when the Castle was one of the strongest in England, and, with the town walls, made Bristol, in the words of the *Gesta Stephani*, 'the most strongly fortified of all its cities'.

The 1989 excavation of the keep of Bristol Castle also yielded a number of stone, bone and pottery items from the time of Earl Robert's recon-struction in the twelfth century. These included half a spindle whorl, made of chalk and decorated with turned grooves, and a bone pin, irregular in cross-section, the head of which was roughly semi-circular, flat, and decorated with a pattern of crossed lines incised into it, slightly bulging at the beginning of the taper to the point. This part also contained traces of decoration; a flat bone strip, possibly a comb's connecting plate, in which were found traces of iron rivets and decorated with a row of concentric circles on one face; part of what may originally have been a bone whistle or flute, roughly trimmed at its unbroken end; and a fragment of bone, the original function of which is unknown, but which had been roughly pared on all sides.

During excavation, 1,064 shards of mostly late eleventh- and early twelfth-century pottery were recovered from the debris used to fill the *motte* ditch.Fifty-five per cent of this material came from pottery composed of the BPT 5 fabric, a hard, well-fired ware containing a fine, chalky grit, rare iron ores and chalks, used in cooking pots and a few bowls between 1080-1120; the BPT 10 fabric, a hard, soapy ware, grey in colour, containing limestone, quartz and rare iron ores, and also used to manufacture cooking pots between 1080-1120, comprised an additional 22 per cent of the material. Most remarkable of the material in BPT 5 was the rim of a pitcher, a form of pottery which previously had not been seen in that fabric. The remaining 23 per cent was composed of BPT 18, a hard, grey ware from north-west Wiltshire, oxidised, with plentiful inclusions of oolitic limestone, used in the manufacture of tripod pitchers from 1080-1200; BPT 17 and 18c, both quartz gritted wares from south-east Wiltshire, and dating from the same period, the one used in cooking pots while the other was used in tripod pitchers, as well as the early post-conquest wares BPT 20, characterised by a hard sandy fabric used in cooking pots, with a large proportion of quartz and limestone and spalling on the internal surfaces, and BPT 115, a hard fabric, gritted with quartz mixed with shell and limestone, also used in cooking pots. Both these type of clay pots commence at 1070, though BPT 115 ceased production in 1100 while BPT 20 finally fell out of fashion 20 years later. There were also 48 shards of BPT 309, a late Saxon cooking pot fabric dating from 950-1080, a hard, grey material, buff on its surface and mixed with limestone, calcite, sandstones, mudstones, chert, and quartz; and four shards of BPT 3, a hard, quartz gritted cooking pot fabric with a moderate mixture of limestone and a little shell, produced from 1000-70. BPT 3 was probably the ancestor of BPT 115, while BPT 309 gradually evolved into BPT 10, from which it is often difficult to distinguish. The excavation also produced a small quantity of Ham Green Ware, in the fabric BPT 114, dating from the early twelfth century, and two shards of BPT 26, a jug fabric produced at Pill between 1120-60. There is the distinct possibility that the Ham Green Ware was an intrusion into these levels and did not properly belong in that location. If that is the case, then the *motte* ditch and its pottery fill can be dated to before 1120. If the Ham Green ware shards genuinely belong in that location, then most of the pottery in the group, and the destruction of the ditch itself, dates from the second quarter of the twelfth century.

A smaller amount of twelfth-century and residual Saxo-Norman pottery was recovered from the Castle's *garderobe* chute. The fabrics there also included the twelfth-century proto-Ham Green Ware BPT 114 (which probably came from a total of three pots), BPT 26, BPT 32, a Ham Green

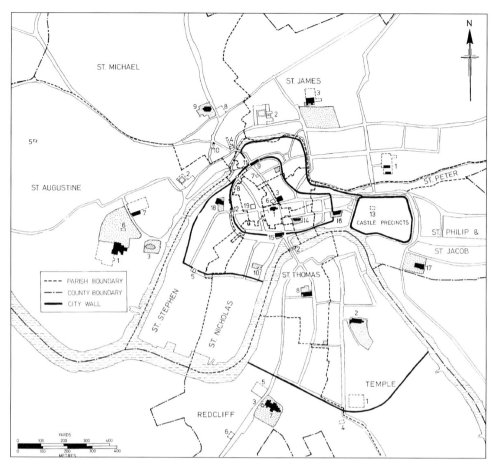

**40** *The churches of the County of Bristol.* Courtesy of D. Dawson, drawing by Barbara Cumby

cooking pot fabric produced between 1120-1300, and seven residual shards of Saxo-Norman fabrics.

The individual shards of pottery themselves incorporated 13 shards of BPT 5 ware, eight of which were from jars, including one which had been tall and hard-fired. Four of them had internal folds, while one had an internal bevel. Another had been internally decorated with wavy combing. Yet another of the rims was decorated with beading. One of the jars was tall, externally rounded but again with an internal fold. The other shards of this ware came from cooking pots, one of which, of poor workmanship, had a thumbed inner edge, while that of another pot, made in a very thin fabric, was shallow with a grooved top. Like some of the jars, it had a slight internal fold; one was the tall, flaring rim of a pitcher decorated with a grooved external bead. One of the pieces in this ware was a flat base sharply angled, possibly from a dish. One of the cooking pot rims in this ware was marked by a slight concavity below its edge.

**Key**

*Within the walls*

1 Parish church of All Saints
2 Chapel of the Assumption of the Virgin Mary
3 Parish church of Christchurch
5 Chapel of St Clement
6 Parish church of St Ewen
7 Chapel of St George
8 Chapel of St Giles
9 Parish church of St John the Baptists
10 Chapel of St John the Evangelist
11 Parish church of St Lawrence
12 Parish church of St Leonard
13 Chapel of St Martin
14 Parish church of St Mary le Port
15 Parish church of St Nicholas
16 Parish church of St Peter
18 Parish church of St Stephen
19 Parish church of St Werburgh

*Without the walls: the suburbs of St Augustine's and St Michael's*

1 Abbey of St Augustine (Augustinian)
2 Carmelite Friary
3 Parish church of St Augustine the Less
4 Hospital of St Bartholomew
5 Chapel of St Brendan
6 Chapel of St Jordan
7 Hospital of St Mark

8 Nunnery of St Mary Magdalen
9 Parish church of St Michael
10 Hospital chapel of the Three Kings of Cologne

*Without the Walls: the suburb of St James'*

1 Blackfriars (Dominican)
2 Greyfriars (Franciscan)
3 Priory and parish church of St James (Benedictine)

*Without the walls: the suburb of SS Philip and Jacob*

4 Hospital of the Holy Trinity and St George
17 Parish church of SS Philip and Jacob

*The suburbs south of the river: St Thomas', Redcliffe and Temple*

1 Austen Friars (Augustinian)
2 Temple church (Knights Templar, later Knights Hospitaller)
3 Chapel of the Holy Spirit
4 Friary of the Sack
5 Hospital of St John the Baptist
6 Hospital of St Mary Magdalen
7 Chapelry of St Mary Redcliffe
8 Chapelry of St Thomas

There were also six cooking pot rims in BPT 10, three of which were decorated with an external bead. One of these was deeply marked by a thumbprint on its inner edge. Another had a slight internal fold and what may have been a very faint external groove, while the sixth was tall and slightly curved at its top, the external edge of which was sharply inclined. There was also a cooking pot rim of BPT 17 fabric, curved with a thumbed edge, and marked with soot on its exterior; and two shards of BPT 18 and BPT 18c respectively. The fragment from BPT 18 was the tall, flaring rim of a tubular spouted pitcher, decorated at its neck with a beaded cord, and glazed dark green. The fragment of BPT 18c was a strap handle, decorated by three strips pressed into the clay by the potter's thumb. The fabric of this pot was heavily gritted with quartz. There was also part of a cooking pot, possibly of Ham Green Ware, in BPT 32. This had a sagging base, which had, nevertheless, been trimmed. Its rim was angular and everted, the edge of which again had been decorated by thumbing. There were also three

**41** *Medieval church sites surveyed archaeologically in Bristol.* Courtesy of D. Dawson, drawing by Barbara Cumby

**Key**

*Abbots Leigh (Somerset)*
1 Chapelry of Holy Trinity

*Bedminster (Somerset)*
1 Hospital of St Catherine Brightbow
2 Parish Church of St John the Baptist
3 Knowle Chapel

*Bishopsworth (Somerset)*
1 chapel
2 Chapel of St Peter Bishport

*Brislington (Somerset)*
1 Chapel of St Anne
2 Chapelry of St Luke

*Clifton (Gloucestershire)*
1 Parish church of St Andrew

*Henbury (Gloucestershire)*
1 Chapel of St Blaise

2 Chapelry of St Laurence
3 Parish church of St Mary the Virgin
4 Chapelry of St Thomas

*Horfield (Gloucestershire)*
1 Chapelry of the Holy Trinity

*Stapleton (Gloucestershire)*
1 Chapelry of the Holy Trinity

*Westbury (Gloucestershire)*
1 Parish church of the Holy Trinity
2 Westbury College
1a Chapel of St Lambert

*Whitchurch (Somerset)*
1 Chapelry of St Gregory (modern church of
   St Nicholas)
2 Filwood Chapel

shards in BPT 114 proto-Ham Green Ware. These had been fired very hard; their rims were slightly everted. One also had a slight internal ledge, while the top and neck of the other was grooved instead. The third had been left plain. All three came from cooking pots, although one may, instead, have originally been a jar.

There were seven shards of BPT 309. Four of these were the rims of cooking pots. Two of them were internally slightly concave, while the inside of another was marked with a wide, shallow indentation. This rim was also slightly everted, while one of the concave rims was decorated with an external bead. One of the pots recovered in this ware was simply a collection of shards, decorated with wavy combing and circular stamped cross-hatch designs. The other two fragments were handles, one knob, one lug, both of which bore stamped designs. The knob and lug handles and the bodies of their pots were decorated with diamond patterns, though the stamp used on the lug-handled pot had been ovoid. Although this is only a narrow example of the type of pottery produced in the fabrics found at the Castle, it nevertheless gives an idea of the type of domestic wares current in the area both before and after the Conquest.

# 10 Religious architecture

The most physically enduring part of Bristol's Norman architectural heritage is its religious buildings. Although the Castle and domestic housing have long since been demolished and built over, some small fraction of the City's Norman religious foundations have survived down to the present day. The Normans were responsible for founding and rebuilding upwards of 19 religious houses, including monasteries and chapels in the Bristol area from the time of the Conquest in 1066 to the foundation of the Plantagenet dynasty in 1154. None of these, however, has survived the vicissitudes of the intervening centuries wholly intact. A number have vanished after falling victim to fires, bomb damage, redundancy and urban redevelopment, while many of the others were extensively rebuilt in the fourteenth, fifteenth and nineteenth centuries in line with new trends in church architecture and the pressures of serving a changing congregation in a living community. Nevertheless, some still retain features from their Norman past, or have been the subject of archaeological investigations that have shed rather more light on this stage of their development. The survival of the Romanesque style until c.1200 also means that later churches, such as St Nicholas at Whitchurch, founded in 1166-7, still show important Norman features and can serve as a guide to the original glories of their lost counterparts elsewhere in the City.

In the City itself, St Mary le Port, St Ewen, All Saints, St James, St Augustine the Less and Holy Cross in Temple Fee have all shown traces of the original Norman structures, even if, in the case of Holy Cross, the early church was in a style far removed from the Norman, or even mainstream European architectural tradition. Just outside the historic centre of the Norman City, the church of St Philip and St Jacob, or Pip and Jay's as it is known to Bristolians, and founded to serve the nascent trading suburb of Old Market, also has links to the Normans. Although the earliest mention of the church dates from around 1191-3 when the Bishop of Worcester confirmed its possession by Tewkesbury Abbey, a twelfth-century tomb slab, originally in the chancel but now removed, displayed the same nailhead design as adorns the gatehouse of Bristol Cathedral. This suggests that it was built roughly at the same time, before the abbey's final dedication in 1170. While not necessarily built during the Norman dynasty, the slab nevertheless is part of the Romanesque architectural tradition, which they introduced. Outshining these by far, though, is the former Augustinian Abbey of Bristol Cathedral, whose

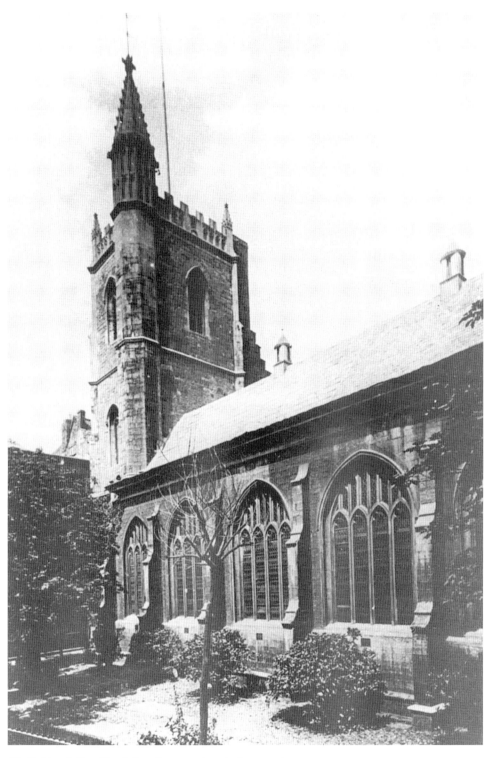

**42** *St Mary le Port Church from the approach to the Saxon settlements*

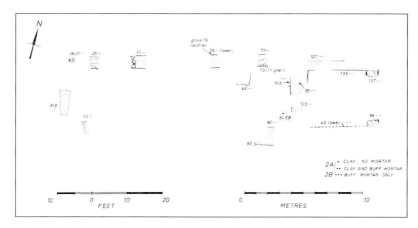

**43** *Norman remains from St Mary le Port.* Courtesy of Prof. P. Rahtz

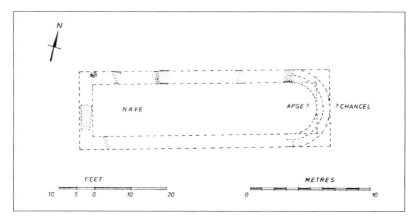

**44** *Conjectured plan of Norman church, St Mary le Port.* Courtesy of Prof. P. Rahtz

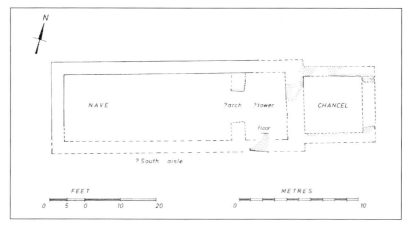

**45** *Conjectured plan of second phase of Norman church, St Mary le Port.* Courtesy of Prof. P. Rahtz

fabric retains significant portions of the original Norman architecture, especially in its Chapter House.

Of the early churches of Bristol, St Peter's, whose remains in Peter Street now occupy part of the eastern end of Castle Park, was burnt out by bombing in 1940, though its ruins have been preserved as a monument. These are mostly medieval and later, with only a portion of the west tower preserving part of the eleventh-century structure. A similar fate tragically befell St Mary le Port, which was also destroyed by bombing that same year although, unlike its neighbour, it was afterwards completely demolished with the exception of the fifteenth-century tower. The ruins did, however, yield much important archaeological evidence after its investigation in 1962-3 by Dr Philip Rahtz, not least because it has so far been the only parish church in the City to be so excavated.

Although reconstruction of the earliest Anglo-Saxon church on the site has been necessarily tentative because of the fragmentary nature of the evidence, rather more can be said of the later Norman church, not least because of a direct continuity between the structures built during this period of the church's construction and the architecture of the later church. It was during this period of St Mary le Port's long history, roughly from 1140-70, that the recognisable form of the medieval church began to take shape in two phases of building work, which saw the Norman church modified by an extension further east, and the addition of a chancel. In both phases the church was built largely of Brandon Hill Grit with smaller amounts of Pennant Sandstone, bound with a buff sandy mortar and sand, marl, or red or brown sandy clay, and possibly re-using the Saxon foundation under the arch of the eastern tower. With a minimum length of approximately 18.7m and a width of 4.3m, this church, like its predecessor, also lacked an aisle.

The archaeological evidence for the possible shape of the eastern end of the church is ambiguous, and may indicate three additional phases of construction within this period of the church's history. The foundations at the north-west end of the church appear to be turning south towards the remains of the eastern wall, possibly indicating that there was an apse here. If so, then the wall would narrow at this point, forming a slight neck before reaching the apse itself. On the other hand, it is also likely that the foundations interpreted as part of an apse may actually have been part of a squared end. These alternatives are not mutually exclusive, however. It is possible that the church was originally apsidal, only for it to be rebuilt as a squared end, in which case the later modifications to the east end were merely the later stages of a lengthy process of remodelling which continued through this stage of the church's history. Regardless of the particular type of the east end, it may also have included a chancel approached through the nave at the western end of the Church.

During the second phase of construction work, a new chancel, set back 19.6-23.6in (0.5-0.6m) from the wall of the nave, and internally 4.75m square, was built extending from the east end of the earlier church building, approached through an arch linking it to a space of 5.5 by 3.5m, possibly underneath a tower. This was approached from the nave through an arch 2.5m in diameter. Although a south wall or arcade later developed along the line of the southern part of the arch, there is no evidence of a corresponding foundation for it opposite those of the northern piers during the Norman period. Its existence, however, is not entirely impossible as the foundations for this section of the church take a turn to the north before reaching the chancel. Considerations of symmetry, suggesting that the chancel was also set back from the nave wall by the same amount on its southern side, and the evidence of a robber trench and foundation on the south side of the nave appear to indicate that its southern wall had been moved so that it became 5.5m in width and, with the separation of the possible tower section by an arch, about 14m in length.

Apart from these modifications, much of the north and west walls of the church remained intact. Amongst the material excavated from the Norman church was a fragment of a stone capital, roughly 18 by 4 by 3.9in (46 by 10.4 by 9.9cm), decorated on its left and upper edge of one face with a pattern of interlinked rings bordered on its upper edge by a line of small pyramidal squares, in turn bordered by a line roughly 0.1 to 0.15in (3 to 4mm) in diameter. Associated with this phase, or the earlier Saxon church under the eastern part of the nave was a cist burial, in which the remains were interred in a tomb composed of end, side and covering slabs of pennant sandstone. Although cist burials in St Mary le Port may have continued after the Norman period, their appearance here suggests a connection with the other cist burials around early Bristol, particularly those at St James and St Augustine the Less.

The area around the church also yielded a wealth of pottery fragments from the Norman period. These include shards of BPT one, two, three, four, 17 and 20, fabrics. BPT one is a light but hard, laminated fabric, tempered with small stones, limestone and quartz. Many of the pots found at St Mary le Port were given separate, broader classifications for the type of fabric used. The categories used for the St Mary le Port pottery consisted of A, a series of early medieval wares, mostly used in cooking pots, containing moderate amounts of grit, mostly with grey cores and buff to brown surfaces, though the surfaces of a few are a dark grey or oxidised reddish-brown; B, a series, of hard, gritty fabrics; and C, a similar hard, but sandy fabric, exclusively used in the manufacture of drinking vessels similar to cups. There were also a series of early medieval glazed wares, fragments of late Stamford ware and a type similar to Winchester ware and Fabric H, a moderately hard, gritty but smooth fabric used in producing cooking pots.

The pottery fragments in Fabric A, dating from the Norman period included a shard from a squat, undecorated cooking pot with a simple rim, similar to BPT two or three ware; several shards from hand-finished pots thrown on a small wheel, with sagging bases, but with slightly differing rims.

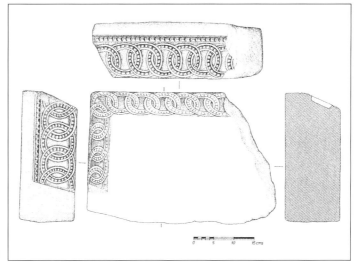

**46** *Norman capital from St Mary le Port.* Courtesy of Prof. P. Rahtz

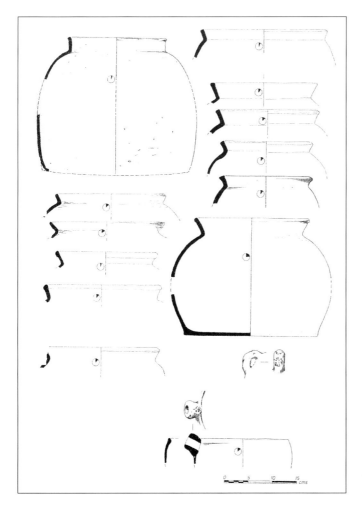

**47** *Saxon and Norman pottery, St Mary le Port.* Courtesy of Prof. P. Rahtz

These are frequently, but not always, everted. The shards of pottery with this type of rim includes a simple, unornamented example, one whose rim was decorated by impressions made on its outer face by the manufacturer's finger-nails; a fragment of rim decorated with a strongly distinct, but simple bead; fragments of a pot with a wide, sagging base; and fragments of another pot with an everted rim. The pottery fragments without such a rim include a shard with both faces reduced, a remarkable feature in itself as this is quite rare; a shard with a simple beaded rim; another decorated by simple beading on the rim, whose neck rose almost vertically and the body of which may have been finished by hand using a coarse cloth or brush; another whose rim thickened, but with a similar vertical neck; a similarly shaped vessel with a vertical neck decorated with a strong external bead, produced by a groove along the inside of the rim; a vessel characterised by the emergence of the neck from the main body in a gentle curve, with the inside of the rim slightly hollowed and the exterior decorated with a slight bead; another vessel with a beaded rim and vertical neck; another pot with an internal groove at the top of the rim, exter-nally decorated with beading and with a straight neck; and a pot with a wide, slightly sagging base with a vertical neck and decorated with a small bead. This fabric included a number of shards with parallels in the 'Norman' pottery found at the Pithay, though their absence from the *motte* ditch at the Castle site strongly indicates that they are actually Anglo-Saxon. These pots all have simple, everted rims, though there are differences in decoration. One

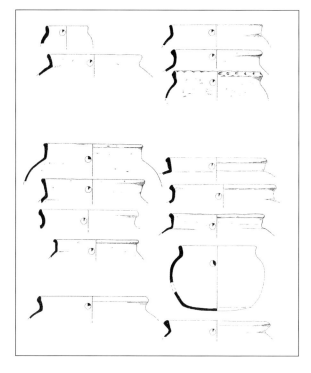

**48** *Norman pottery, St Mary le Port.* Courtesy of Prof. P. Rahtz

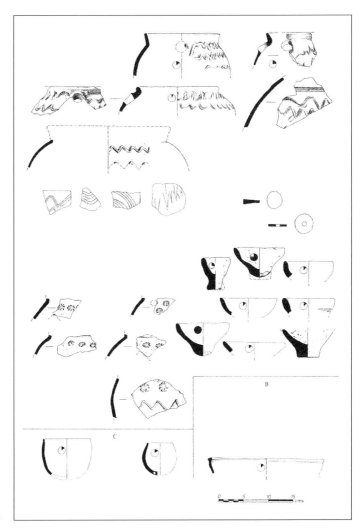

**49** *Norman pottery and lamps, St Mary le Port.* Courtesy of Prof. P. Rahtz

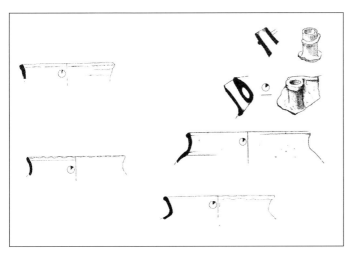

**50** *Norman Pottery, St Mary le Port.* Courtesy of Prof P. Rahtz

**51**  *Southern Romanesque façade, All Saints*

fragment is quite plain, while the rim of another has some swelling on the outer face. Another pot possesses a rim, the top of which has been cut at a sharp angle; four other pots have a bead on their outer and inner face, though in two the beading is only slight. This is a feature which is confined to the inside of another, similar pot, while on another it only occurs on its outer face. Also found in this fabric were spouts and handles from tripod pitchers. These included a small looped handle, the loop of which was 2.28in (58mm), decorated on its upper surface with two stamped rosettes; the spout of a bowl, the upper surface of which is decorated with a single rosette stamp and whose rim possesses a simple internal bead and the remains of a spouted pitcher with a simple pouring hole at the top of its shoulder, which, as well as the pot's body, was decorated by heavy scoring made before firing. The pot's internal surface was heavily pitted, possibly by whatever it was used to contain, while the outside was oxidised in a light-brown slip. The rim was, like many of the other pots, slightly everted; fragments of another vessel, the shoulder of which was ornamented with multipoint tooling, again done before firing, with a simple pouring hole just below its rim, which was also quite simple. Like the preceding pot, this too had a heavily pitted interior and an exterior coated in a light brown slip; a shard from the body of a large pot, again decorated by scoring. In this instance the fabric was that of the BPT 20 pottery found at Bristol Castle. Several of the shards had been decorated in chevron, combed and stamped designs, including a shard from another pot's shoulder, decorated with two scribed chevron bands; a fragment from another pot decorated in two sets of chevron combing; a fragment of pottery decorated by combing in wide, wavy lines; a fragment of similar pottery, again decorated with combing though this time circular; another pottery fragment with a high quartz content, decorated in uncombed chevron scoring; the clay of all of the last four pots had been oxidised. There was also a fragment of a pot decorated with a corner of chevron scribing and two stamped rosettes; a possible fragment of a spouted pitcher, decorated by two rectilinear stamps; a fragment decorated in three rosette stamps; and yet another fragment, this time with only two such stamps; and a fragment of pottery decorated with two rosette stamps, above and below which are a pattern of chevron scribing. Also composed of this clay were an unfinished counter, possible spindle-whorl and a number of lamps. These included two small lamps, one of which was of an identical type of clay to the BPT three fabric found at the Castle; another lamp, of the same fabric, was also found, with a smooth finish to its exterior; the smooth, exterior rim only of another lamp; and another lamp, again with a smooth exterior, the body of which thinned underneath the rim.

In Fabric B were found fragments of a pot with an internal and external bead, and a simple everted rim. The cups in Fabric C were 2.04 and 3.38in (5.2 and 8.6cm) in diameter. Found in Fabric E were the spouts and rims of pitchers, glazed olive green, of a kind comparable to wares from south-east Wiltshire. One of these pitchers differed from its fellow in that its spout leaned forward from the main body of the vessel, with a thin strip of clay running from its top to the rest of the vessel across the intervening space. This was similar to types found at Wareham Castle. Its fellow was more similar to types found at Gloucester. Fabric G produced two shards from the bodies of pots decorated with a very glossy, iridescent and finely crackled glaze. In Fabric H

**52** *Northern Romanesque façade, All Saints*

were found fragments of a pot with an everted neck and internal and external bead, of the same type as BPT 4 pottery found in the *motte* ditch at Bristol Castle; a fragment of pottery with a wide, slightly sagging base and simple bead on its exterior face, and slightly everted rim; and a fragment of pottery similar to that used in tripod pitchers, again with a slightly everted rim and finger crimping on the top surface and internal ledge, similar to the BPT fabrics six to 11. Also found in the Norman levels were the fossils of two sea urchins, possibly kept either as curiosities or charms, a tantalising clue to how medieval people regarded and interpreted the remains of creatures from the remote geological past.

Long before the destruction of these two churches, however, St Ewen in Broad Street and St Werburgh's in Corn Street had already been demolished during the nineteenth century as part of a programme of municipal works. The chancel of St Werburgh was destroyed in 1760 when Small Street was widened, and although the rest survived for another 118 years, it too eventually succumbed during development in 1878. Some parts of the church did manage to survive this process, however. The tower and other parts of the church were moved to Mina Road and incorporated into a new bank. Similarly, the church of St Ewen was demolished somewhat earlier, around 1824, to make room for the new council house and its cellars. There were some compensations to its destruction, however, as during the work fragments of the church's twelfth century architecture were discovered, most notably a small, early Norman window.

Although no longer used as a place of worship, All Saints in Corn Street has not been subjected to municipal development and currently survives as the education centre for the Anglican diocese of Bristol. Transferred to the ownership of St Augustine's Abbey, now the cathedral by Earl Ranulf of

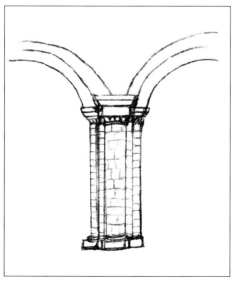

**53** *Romanesque pillar, St James' Priory*

**54** *St Nicholas, Whitchurch*

Chester, some time before 1153, All Saints contains a rich mixture of architectural features from the fifteenth and eighteenth centuries, and even from c.1916. All that remains of the Norman church, however, is the core of the tower, and, more visibly, the two bays either side of the western end of the nave. These have relatively simple, unornamented arches, possibly dating from c.1140, supported by round columns with scalloped capitals.

Moving away from the historic centre of Bristol, the churches of St Augustine the Less, St James and Holy Cross at Temple Fee are no less interesting. Although the church of St Augustine the Less was effectively destroyed by wartime bombing, and its ruins finally cleared away in 1972, archaeological investigation of St Augustine the Less nevertheless revealed a wealth of information. The twelfth century church may have been built to accommodate the abbey's canons while they were awaiting its completion, possibly c.1148 when, according to the Newland Roll, the monastery's first abbot, Richard, was inducted. Despite this, the church was to enjoy a long career into the twentieth century, becoming a parish church by 1291. This early church, constructed both of stone and timber, was small, 9.2m long and 3.8m wide internally, approached through a doorway of oolitic limestone blocks. This door and its rebate to the south measured 37.7in by 34in (96cm by 85cm). The doorjambs themselves survived to a height of 23.6in (60cm) from the foundations of the wall, which measured 2m by 1.1m by 29.5in (75cm). These were constructed of Brandon Hill Grit

111

surrounding a core of rubble intermixed with sand and clay, and with internally projecting footings, similar to the contemporary Norman domestic building at Tower Lane. A pale yellow sandy mortar was used to cement the base of the south-west doorjambs and the upper courses of thenorth-west wall. Although the building's east end andnorth-east corner had been destroyed by the construction of the later medieval chancel walls and post-medieval burial vaults, one corner was found in the north-west, with a trench marking the robbing of other related stonework extending east from the north wall for 2.7m. Parallel to the northern robber trench, a second extended eastwards from the doorway for 7.2m. The remains of the foundation of a partition wall, running north to south, was also found 32.2in (82cm) east of the doorway, with the possible remains of a second internal wall running a further 3m east of this, forming a bay 2.9 by 3.8m. This possible two-bay plan may show a similarity to the design of the vaulted chancel, also Norman, but still surviving, at St Michael's church in Compton Martin. Later in the twelfth century the church was further modified by the construction of a western extension and the insertion of two acoustic jars, possibly set below the timber stalls and intended to amplify sounds from the choir.

Although the church and its grounds continued to be used for burials, several dating from the thirteenth to fourteenth centuries, none appear to have been specifically identified as belonging to the Norman period. This may be due to the lack of dating material found with the remains, the distur-

**55** *Norman font, St Nicholas, Whitchurch*

**56** *Norman sanctuary and chancel, St Nicholas, Whitchurch*

bance of the burial sites in the eighteenth century when the area underneath
the east end of the north aisle in the church was cleared prior to its extension,
and the construction of the Georgian terrace in Deanery Road, the subsequent building of the Royal Hotel at the east end of the terrace in 1868 and
road-widening at the east end of College Green, and the sheer density of
some of the burials, such as those under the nineteenth century vestry in the
south-east corner of the church, where the earth had been disturbed so
frequently that it was impossible to discern the outlines of the individual
graves, many of which in any case cut into each other.

For many years before its redundancy the former priory church of St James,
founded in 1137, claimed to be Bristol's oldest surviving parish church. It too
has suffered the effects of changes in architectural fashion and the destruction
of the Dissolution, so that what survives is the liturgically less important part
of the original priory church, the remains of the rest of the monastic complex
lying underneath the bus station. The subsequent alterations to the original
Norman church include a fourteenth- to fifteenth-century tower, and a
seventeenth-century south aisle, while the present north aisle dates from 1864.
The remaining Norman features include a wheel window set into the west
wall, possibly dating from c.1160, consisting of a pattern of eight circular
windows surrounding a central window, each surrounded and interlaced with
a rope moulding, the pattern as a whole surrounded by a circular border of
four chevron, zigzag, lines, which are in turn surrounded by a more conven-

tional circular border. This is set above three round-headed windows, themselves set into a row of arches, again decorated with the same zigzag pattern and West Country Romanesque interlace design, below which is the church's doorway. These three windows somewhat resemble the Norman west end of Llandaff Cathedral, another of the earl's foundations and the chief church in his lands. Although the eastern bay belonging to the monastic church was demolished after the dissolution, its *pulpitum* wall and the other five bays of the Norman nave still survive. This still retains the clerestorey of simple, round-headed windows, and arcades of round, slender columns, each possessing four shafts, which bear the shafts and arches supporting the timber roof. These arches, although possessing scalloped capitals, have no mouldings.

Originally the church may have been cruciform in plan, the transepts of which may also have possessed chapels on their eastern sides, as well as a short extension containing the presbytery possibly leading to a round-ended sanctuary, perhaps similar to the earliest east end of the Norman church of St Mary le Port. It appears that the eastern part of the church was entered by an arch decorated by at least six shafted orders, (the recessed stages into which Norman and Gothic arches were cut), as at the cathedrals of Hereford and Llandaff. Surprisingly, considering its status as a cell of Tewkesbury, St James shows no influence from this abbey in its construction. It is also likely that the western part of the church was built later than its monastic buildings, in which Earl Robert was buried after his death in 1148. The usual sequence in the construction of monastic churches was for the high altar, monks' choir and most of the chapels to be built first, followed by the rest of the nave. Sometimes the interval during the construction of the different parts of the church, between those occupied by the monks and those for the lay public, was so great that quite significant changes in style had occurred in the meantime. This appears to have been the case at St James, where the west wall's features may be somewhat later than those of the rest of the church.

The priory's burial ground was quite extensive. Although no trace of the western cloister buildings was found during the excavation in 1975, due to disturbance caused by the construction of the heating systems' ducting, investigation of the burial ground at Cannon Street yielded over 30 inhumations. Apart from the Saxon head-niche graves, these included internments in which coffins had been used. Although these had long since decayed, the nails used in their construction remained to mark their existence. These later, monastic burials were more closely aligned east to west than the earlier Saxon material, and the number of burials increased towards the western end of the site. The main east-facing section of the burial ground was marked by the disturbance of the graves. Some burials cut into each other, and many had been removed or seriously damaged by the construction of later features. The coffin burials cut into the earlier head-niche graves, as did two circular pits 35.4in (90cm) in diameter and 19.68in (50cm) deep, the purpose of which remains unknown. Running north to south across the site was a line of four post holes, three of which cut into the fill of the head-niche graves. Considering the theological importance of the consecrated ground of the church itself, it is unsurprising that the western end of the burial ground nearest the church should be the most intensively used.

One of the most curious, if not outright outlandish, of all Bristol's medieval churches was undoubtedly the Templar church of Holy Cross at Temple Fee. Another church destroyed by bombing in 1940, its remains have been a public park since it was taken into guardianship in 1960. Although most of the visible church dates from the late fourteenth century, it nevertheless contains the foundations of the original Templar church built after the order had been given this part of Bedminster in 1118. Discovered underneath the church floor during renovation work and excavated by A.D. Saunders in 1872, these suggested an oval church 27.5m by 18.6m, built in the form of a rotunda containing a central nave enclosed in an ambulatory with an apsidal chancel, a design typical of many of the order's churches. As time wore on, the monastic complex at Temple fee became the order's administrative centre for its lands in the south-west. The design of the church was taken from that of the Armenian churches the order encountered during its career in the Crusades. As such, the church was a strange outpost of the Middle East, set amongst the damp expanses of Bristol's marshlands, the embodiment of an armed and militant papacy. A little distance away from the church, the remains of a large twelfth-century hall have also been found. Although it is unclear from the remains who the proprietor might have been, its proximity to the church suggests it might well have belonged to the order, despite the extreme asceticism under which most of the knights lived. It is quite possible that the hall might well have been the administrative centre of the Order's lands in the city, and the place where they received and negotiated with dignitaries from within and outside Bristol.

Although the church's exotic design may well have struck contemporary Bristolians as outlandish, perhaps even sinister, the order does not seem to have acquired the same sinister reputation for Satanism and homosexuality prevalent in France. Edward II frankly disbelieved the accusations, and although the order was eventually dissolved in England in 1312, only two out of the order's 144 knights were tortured and most of their lands passed smoothly into the hands of their brother order, the Hospitallers. This was true also of Bristol, where Temple church appears in Philip de Thame's report to the Hospitallers' Grand Master, Elyan de Villanova in 1338 as a small church valued at four marks. Nevertheless, the church has over the years become the subject of an urban legend. The traditional explanation for the pronounced lean of the Perpendicular tower, in this case a definite misnomer, is that the Templars, on their acquisition of the property, arrogantly ejected the existing clergy. In revenge, the local residents did not inform them that the land was marshy and the earlier church had been built on rafts to counteract possible subsidence. Thus the Templars erected their own church without taking this into account, and so suffered the consequences as the church tower gradually sank, falling out of alignment so that at the top the tower is 5ft 4.187in (1.63 m) away from the vertical. In fact the tower dates from long after the Templars' dissolution, its construction probably beginning in 1389 according to a bequest by Bernard Obeleye, after the Order's rotunda had been demolished in preparation for the construction of an aisled hall nave. The legend may reflect the resentment of the late fourteenth-century parishioners against the destruction of what by that time was no doubt a familiar and much-loved church. Subsequent generations confused the parochial clergy at whose behest the church was demolished with the Templars, whose memory was kept alive in the district's name. It may also reflect Reformation anti-clericalism directed against the monastic orders, an atmosphere of religious hostility, which may either have generated the legend, or singled out the Templars as the villainous architects of the leaning tower.

Such attitudes appear to be an anachronism. The Templars, although marking off their own particular demesnes from their neighbours, nevertheless were keenly interested in exploiting their lands to the full, and made full use of the agricultural and trading resources available to them. Plots of land were rented out to incoming tradesmen and merchants, who would surely not have immigrated to the area had the Order's government proven especially onerous. Furthermore, the Order represented independence from the secular lords ruling the City proper, an independence that was jealously guarded, as the resentment of the burgesses of Redcliffe against the union of their suburb with Bristol shows. While the assimilation of Temple Fee into Bristol appears to have proceeded without comparable incident to the Redcliffe episode, suburban pride here was strong enough for the citizens to quarrel with those

**57** *Norman font, St Augustine's, Whitchurch, showing chisel marks of now lost shields*

**58** *Trefoil capital, chevron arch and Romanesque vaulting, abbey gatehouse*

of Redcliffe and Bedminster. Whatever later generations may consider about the Templars, in Bristol at least the order does not seem to have been particularly resented and, in its foundation of this important mercantile district, contributed immensely to the City's growing prosperity.

Further south, at the very fringes of the modern City, the parish of Whitchurch shows some fascinating examples of Norman architecture in the churches of St Nicholas and St Augustine. Although St Nicholas, like St James, is today a splendid mixture of medieval and Victorian architectural features, it still retains part of its original Norman structure. The church itself was granted in 1166-72 to Keynsham Abbey at the time of its construction by Earl William of Gloucester, and is a typically Norman cruciform church with a central, crossing tower. The south aisle, south-east chapel and west end of the nave are fifteenth century, as is the north porch and the tower's pyramid roof. The chancel is thirteenth century early English. The north doorway and tower, however are Norman, though with the addition of perpendicular bell-openings and parapet to the latter, as is the north transept and its roof. The church also retains a square Norman font. Although these later additions make it difficult to imagine the details of the original Norman church, nevertheless it still gives an indication of its original appearance, and so gives some idea of what the area's other Norman churches may have looked like, particularly as many of them, including St Mary le Port, were also granted to Keynsham abbey at the same time.

Also of interest is the Norman font at St Nicholas' sister church of St Augustine. While this church is very modern indeed, built in the early 1970s to serve the new Bridge Farm estate, the bowl of the font is Norman, taken from a now demolished church in East Lydford in Somerset, though other

117

**59** *Door to the twelfth-century night stairs, Bristol Cathedral*

sources, suggest it came originally from St Augustine the Less. It differs from the standard Norman design in that it is round, like the earlier Saxon fonts, rather than square, which, if not indicating that it is quite early in date, suggests that it came from an area in which the Anglo-Saxon religious architectural tradition was still strong. In its heyday the font was also decorated with a series of shields. These appear to have been removed during Cromwell's *Interregnum*, though their places on the font are still visible through the remaining tool marks made by the chisels. While the font may have its origins outside of Bristol, like St Nicholas' church, it gives an impression of the appearance of similar fonts from the Saxon and Norman period within the City, whilst reminding us that even within the relatively slow pace of change in the Middle Ages, stylistic conventions were fluid and subject to alteration. It also shows that, as living communities, cities such as Bristol expand and change, taking features from beyond their borders in time and space and transforming them into an integral part of their own structure. The Norman font at St Augustine's church demonstrates that, although fossilised, Norman architecture still remains a living part of the modern Christian architectural tradition in this part of the West Country.

Aside from these centres of Christian worship, there is the intriguing possibility that Bristol may also possess an early example of Jewish spirituality in the possible *miqveh*, or Jewish ritual bath, found at Jacob's Wells Road in Clifton. This was discovered during building work on one of the properties set into the cliff. The *miqveh* took the form of a spring in a small cave, approached through a massive freestone doorway with a rebate for a door, whose lintel was inscribed with the Hebrew word '*Zacklim*' meaning 'flowing'. If indeed it is a Jewish ritual spring, then it probably dates to the first half of the twelfth century before the foundation of St Augustine's Abbey and the erection of conduits for the water supply from Brandon Hill.

More recently some doubt has been expressed about the spring's use as a *miqveh*. The cave's dimensions would make it difficult to use as a ritual bath, while Jewish religious buildings and ceremonies were not usually tolerated within such close proximity to places of Christian worship. The *miqveh* is near the bottom of Brandon Hill, at the top of which is the church of St Michael. Furthermore the *miqveh* is of an unusually early date. The only other examples from this period are in Spain and Germany. It is also some little distance away from the historic location of Bristol's Jewry in Tower Lane between the Castle and the town. It may also be that elements of the structure, such as the lintel, may post-date the cave itself, making it unlikely that it does date from this period. Although the Hebrew inscription does strongly argue for a Jewish origin, its use is certainly not confined solely to Judaism. Christians have also, on occasion, included passages in Hebrew on their monuments, though these often date from after the Reformation when the original Hebrew and Greek versions superseded the Latin *Vulgate* as the authoritative Biblical texts. Moreover, the *miqveh* was discovered at a time of particular interest in the history of the Jewish community in Bristol, when there were a series of exhibitions celebrating their presence and culture in the City from the eleventh century onwards, and it has been suggested that this may have biased the interpretation of the structure towards that of a Jewish ritual bath. In so doing, it may also have suggested that Bristol enjoyed an extraordinary climate of tolerance towards non-Christian religious worship, which may, in fact, not have existed. The situation is further clouded by the fact that in their ministry, many leading twelfth-century churchmen defied the prejudice of the time to seek out religious influences from the Jewish community. Stephen Harding sought for authoritative texts of the *Old Testament* among Parisian Jews, while Andrew of St Victor, the prior of the Bristolian abbey's mother-house at Wigmore, and one of the witnesses to the foundation of the abbey at Keynsham, also had engaged in theological debates with Parisian Jewry and incorporated rabbinical methods of exegesis and teachings in his own scriptural commentaries. Keynsham Abbey in particular had a mission to convert the Jews, and at the time of their expulsion from Bristol in 1290 the City possessed not only a *scole Judeorum* or synagogue but also a *domus conversorum* or school for converts established to convert them to Christianity.

The *domus conversorum* is likely to have been the Norman building at Dolphin Street. With walls 2m thick, built directly onto the town wall so that this formed its east wall, the building possessed an undercroft about 10m wide with a window with jamb and cill splays. The building's geographical location, like that of the Parisian outsider groups studied by contemporary French historians, does, however, epitomize their place in medieval society. They were literally marginalized, confined to the town walls. Nevertheless, it also betrays others relationships, close to the centre of royal power. Caught between the town and the Castle, Bristol's medieval Jewry was at once at the fringes of society and at its heart. Their financial and business acumen made them valuable, if not necessarily entirely welcome citizens cultivated by those in power. Although to modern eyes the thickness of the walls is uncomfortably sinister, given the historical prejudice and hostility towards Jews, they are in fact quite typical of twelfth-century stone buildings, perhaps indicating that hostility then was not quite so intense as in later ages. Despite its foundation by the area's two most powerful men, Robert of Gloucester and Robert FitzHarding, it is very unlikely that these missionary efforts were successful in gaining either converts or money.

Given this complex religious situation, it may well be that the Hebrew inscription is actually Christian in origin, carved either as part of the church's mission to the Jews, or else as a later expression of faith in the origins of Christianity in *Old Testament* prophecy. As it stands, the *miqveh* and its inscription offers an intriguing conundrum about religious toleration and pluralism in twelfth-century Bristol.

Outshining all of the Norman parish churches in Bristol, however, is the great abbey, now the Cathedral, of St Augustine, at College Green, founded by Robert Fitzharding in 1140, according to the main documentary source of Abbot Newland's *Roll*, though this probably refers to the commencement of building work. Fitzharding may well have been influenced in his selection of the Victorines as the beneficiaries of his new house by the foundation of their convent, originally at Shobdon, but later settled at Wigmore in Herefordshire. The *Newland Roll* and the cartulary of St Augustine's, or *Red Book*, both mention that the church was dedicated by four bishops in 1146, though the names given in the latter really relate to a dedication which took place 24 years later in 1170. It is possible that the 1146 dedication was that of an unfinished church or temporary accommodation for the canons, possibly that of St Augustine the Less. Two years later on Easter Day, 6 April, 1148, Richard of Warwick was inducted as abbot along with the first six canons. Richard had been a canon at the abbey's mother-house of St Victor in Paris, and shortly after his election as abbot of St Augustine's in Bristol visited the Victorine convent at Wigmore. This visit, although brief, was not without effect. A charter of Robert Fitzharding's son, Nicholas, states that it was during Bishop Alfred's episcopacy in Worcester of 1158-60, that the canons entered their church. The *Newland Roll* states that six canons of Wigmore also entered the new abbey during Alfred's episcopacy, though places it ten years previously at the time of the induction of Abbot Richard, when it is far more likely that they entered the new house c.1159. Although the abbey proper was now sufficiently advanced in its construction to be occupied, it had to wait approximately another 11 years before it was finally dedicated by Bishops

**60** *The abbey gatehouse, showing chevron arch, vaulting and arcading*

Bartholomew of Exeter, Roger of Worcester, Nicholas of Llandaff, and Godfrey of St Asaph in 1170. In the meantime Robert had been gathering royal patronage for his new order. An early charter of Henry II refers to his visit to the City in 1153, while in another charter he recalled the church that he 'helped in his early youth', *ecclesiam …quam inicio iuventutis mee beneficiis*. So closely was Henry associated with the foundation of the abbey through his patronage of FitzHarding that eventually he came to be considered as its co-founder, a belief literally set in stone in an inscription over the abbey's gatehouse, which reads '*Rex Henricus Secundus et Dominus Robertus filius Hardingi filii Regis Daciae huius monasterii primi fundatores exstiterunt*'.

Since its foundation the abbey has undergone much alteration in line with changing architectural fashions and repairs until well into the twentieth century. The last additions to the Cathedral were made by its official architect, George Oatley, and Professor Tristram in the period from the 1930s to the 1950s, when the north porch's inner lobby was built, the west doors glazed, and the nave and choir bosses gilded and the polychrome of the Eastern Lady Chapel improved. The constraints imposed by the abbey's geographical position, perched on a section of ground dropping from north to south and from east to west, also altered its construction from the more usual layout of Augustinian houses, and necessitated the construction of a suitable platform of ground to support the church. The church may have been built in two phases, possibly beginning with the south transept, around

**61** *Detail of arcading, abbey gatehouse*

a cloister 28m square, as parts of the building are considerably more ornate than others, suggesting that these were built after Henry's coronation in 1154, when he was able to add his considerable patronage to augment the more modest buildings made available by FitzHarding's rather more limited funds. The abbey is smaller than the other great Benedictine houses in the medieval diocese, such as Evesham, Tewkesbury, Gloucester and Pershore, and much smaller than the Augustinian house at Cirencester. The first phase saw the construction of the church complex, while the second, included some, if not all of the abbey's domestic buildings, the Chapter House, and the western gateway to the outer courtyard. It is possible, however, that the nave was constructed at the same time as the gateway and Chapter House, as an illustration of a particularly elaborate stepped trefoil capital from the nave in E.W. Godwin's 1863 article on the Cathedral's Romanesque architecture, is identical to some of those surviving in the gatehouse and Chapter House. It is here, in the position of the Chapter House that the influence of the peculiar local geography makes itself felt. Usually Augustinian Chapter Houses were joined to the church transept by a slype, a passageway leading from the cloister to the abbey cemetery. At Bristol Cathedral, however, the Chapter House abuts directly onto the main body of the church, and the slype instead runs south of it. The church was cruciform in plan, about 66m long, and 17m wide, with a transept 34m long by 9m wide. Its walls were 1.5m thick. From the evidence of the Romanesque gable and its round-headed window in the south transept, it appears that the church, like St Mary le Port, was originally built from red Brandon Hill millstone grit. Like its Anglo-Saxon predecessors, the church would have been plastered, though it differed from them in that, from the evidence of surviving plaster fragments from St Alban's Cathedral in Hertfordshire, this was probably white rather than pink.

From the late twelfth-century seal of Abbot John it appears that the church possessed a clerestorey, two transept towers and an aisle with round-headed windows. This latter detail is a matter of considerable debate, as although it has been traditionally assumed that the church at this stage possessed aisles, the architect G.E. Street, when designing the Victorian nave in 1869 noted the existence of a foundation wall on each side of the nave, suggesting that originally it did not in fact have one. The transept towers depicted on the seal may also be erroneous. These may really show staircase towers, such as those on the Romanesque transept of Canterbury Cathedral. The surviving twelfth-century masonry on the wall of the south transept does possess pilaster buttresses, but this does not necessarily indicate that it had a tower situated there. As depicted, the transept towers with their spirelet caps show the distinct influence of Rhenish Romanesque, and if they really existed they may well have been placed closer to the central crossing, as at Robert of Gloucester's great Llandaff Cathedral, rather than flanking the transepts as at Hereford.

A more obvious mistake appears to be the absence of a central crossing tower. This does not appear on the seal, although its presence is certainly indicated by the piers supporting the church's present tower, built broad and thick to support its weight, and which, although cut back from their original twelfth-century form, would originally have been cruciform with shafts attached to the end of each arm. The tower, although heavy, may not have been particularly high. The Victorian architect E.W. Godwin considered that the tower may have been squat with a pyramidal roof, similar to the other, smaller Romanesque churches built by the Normans. It is also possible that the church possessed a pair of belfry towers at the west end as described by William Worcester in his *Itinerary*, and similar to twelfth-century Cistercian abbeys such as Pontigny in Burgundy and Fountains in Yorkshire. Between these, Worcester also describes a Galilee chapel, though no trace of this seems to exist today.

The nave itself had six bays, the last, western bay flanked by towers. The piers for them were spaced 5.5m apart from centre to centre. Abbot John's seal also appears to show a short presbytery limb, with an unaisled eastern bay and probably square-ended according to Augustinian architectural conventions. The nave probably possessed a north door, roughly in the same position as the modern door, opposite which was a door to the cloister, with a second cloister door situated further east, as indicated by doors in similar positions at Ely Cathedral, and in the fabric of Winchester Cathedral. If the nave did indeed have aisles, these would have been elevated in three parts similar to that of St Bartholomew the Great in London.

Despite subsequent alterations, the original plan of the Romanesque transepts appears to have survived, though there may have been apsidal chapels on their eastern sides, which have since been demolished to make room for the Elder Lady and Newton chapels. The Norman pilaster buttresses on the north transept may, however, still be seen beneath the

**62** *Detail of vaulting, abbey gatehouse*

gothic buttress reinforcing the late medieval vaulting, and rising up the eastern wall above the level of the Elder Lady Chapel's roof. Remnants of the original twelfth-century buttressing may also be seen in the south-west corner of the south transept. A Romanesque corbel, also in the south-west corner, gives an indication of the original height of the building, while marks either side of its Romanesque window also show the pitch of the roof. Another window survives above the arch in the east wall leading to the Newton Chapel. Godwin suggested that there may have been three such windows, while the north transept may have possessed two rows of them, similar, but not identical, to Romsey Abbey in Hampshire, where the greater height of the wall allows for three rows of two windows each, rather than the two rows of three windows envisaged by Godwin. The south transept would not have possessed more than one row of these windows because of the proximity of the Chapter House.

Underneath the central tower was situated the choir with the church extending east for a further three bays with an aisle of two bays in width running either side of it. The junction of the first two bays of the arcade running between the chancel and the nave may be indicated by the base of a rectangular pier discovered in 1894. Like the later stages of the contemporary church at St Mary le Port, the church's east end was square, rather than apsidal. Godwin also suggested that both chancel aisles may have possessed altars at their east ends, as well as a *via processionis* running around that end of the church, including the choir and sanctuary. This area may also have been concealed behind a screen with the high altar located at the east end of the nave itself.

Despite the elaborate vaulting in the Chapter House, the original Romanesque church was probably unvaulted, possibly due to the lack of funds. The nine corbel heads, now situated in a stairwell off the aisle of the north choir, are all classic examples of mid-twelfth century south-western English Romanesque, and may therefore have come originally from the western part of the nave which was probably built at this date. They distinctly resemble similar carvings on the arches of Windrush in Gloucestershire, Kilpeck in Herefordshire and Iffley in Oxfordshire, while three are particularly similar to 'beakhead' designs, in which a beak-like snout extends from the face of a monster to curl around a roll-moulding underneath it. These first appeared in their finished form at Reading in the 1130s, and are particularly associated with arches, although they may also serve, amongst other things, as corbel tables, the row of corbels on the eaves of churches, such as those at Clevedon, a dependent house of St Augustine's in Bristol.

The Chapter House was the location for the canons regular meetings during which the abbey's business was discussed, individual duties for the performance of the daily office allocated, and discipline enforced. It originally had seating for 52, but probably far fewer usually attended ordinary meetings, as the number of canons may have been fewer than 30. On the important occasions when representatives from the dependent estates and daughter houses were required to be present, they were permitted to look through the two small openings, each adorned with shafts of Purbeck marble or a similar stone, either side of the main doorway. The use of this architectural device at Bristol predates its later use in the construction of the Galilee chapel at Durham Cathedral between 1170-5 by nearly a decade. The windows were probably originally unglazed, although they could also have possessed shutters. One mid-nineteenth-century commentator stated they also possessed medieval metal grilles, which implied that they might at some point have been glazed in order to need the protection of such metal stanchions.

The Chapter House is approached through an anteroom off the east cloister walk linking it to the main cathedral building. This anteroom is considerably lower than the Chapter House itself to accommodate the passage from the dormitory to the night stairs running above it, in which one of the original twelfth-century wooden doors has recently been discovered. Although the body of both the Chapter House and the anteroom are constructed from the same Brandon Hill Grit as the rest of the Romanesque church, it is concealed beneath ashlar facings. Both round and pointed arches are used in the anteroom's vaulting, the round arches running from north to south and the pointed from east to west, allowing the rectangular anteroom to be suitably decorated without distorting the shape of the round vaulting. A similar, though grander example of the use of two round and two pointed arches, is in the central tower of St Bartholomew the Great in London. Nearer home, a similar scheme can also be seen in the crossing tower of St John's in Devizes. Although only 14ft (4.26m) across, the anteroom itself is fronted by an arcade of three arches, similar to that of Fountains Abbey in Yorkshire and Haughmond in Shropshire, and divided into two aisles of three bays each, terminating in a pair of pillars set against its western wall. Running along the east side is a stone bench, while *sedilia*, the recessed stone seats carved for the clergy, also run along the north and south walls, testifying to the anteroom's original purpose as a lobby for the main Chapter House, and the existence throughout history of people waiting for bureaucratic meetings. The anteroom possesses a quadripartite ribbed vault, the ribs decorated with beaded undersides and broad roll mouldings, and supported centrally by square piers, each with attached shafts. At the centre of the north and south walls, forming a jamb between two *sedilia*, are thin shafts, each rising to a scalloped capital from which emerges two ribs. Knot and foliate bosses decorate the ribs' intersections in the western bays, similar to the crypt at Gloucester. The marble shafts, arches, vault ribs, and moulded and beaded decoration probably date from 1160, though the anteroom's short pillars, square and round shafts and scalloped capitals may be earlier than 1150.

There is some debate over the original dimensions of the Chapter House. Worcester, in his *Itinerary*, states that it was three times longer than it was wide, about 22.5m by 7.5m. This is larger than the Chapter House as it presently stands, even if the anteroom is included in the measurements. Although the Chapter House suffered periodic remodelling between 1714 and the early 1830s, the most drastic episode being the destruction of the eastern wall during the Bristol riots, archaeological investigation has revealed that the original Romanesque building did not extend further than the original east bay, though it is possible that it did possess an apse, possibly included by Worcester in his measurements of the Chapter House. This apse, however, may have been replaced during the Perpendicular period by a square end and a Gothic arch. It is possible, however, that the engraving which appears to support this theory, by J. Britton in his *History and Antiquities of the Abbey and Cathedral Church of Bristol* in 1830, may be inaccurate, and that the Chapter House never possessed an apse. Although contemporary chapter houses show a plethora of shapes, including polygonal, as at Worcester, that of the Cluniac house of Much Wenlock in Shropshire, which is the most similar to Bristol stylistically, is also rectangular. Furthermore, the historian Browne Willis describes a now vanished circular Romanesque window in the east wall, which would also argue against an apse.

The present Chapter House also has a quadripartite ribbed vault rising to a height of 7.5m, and a transverse arch dividing its two bays. Twenty *sedilia* are built along each side of the room, while further seating was no doubt originally ranged along the east side. The ribs are decorated with chevron designs, the diagonal ribs possessing either simple chevrons on one, and with the addition of a central hexagonal foliate design on the other respectively, the chevrons on each rib running in different directions. The chevron pattern of the transverse rib is further elaborated with nailhead designs. At the ribs' intersections are bosses similar to those in the anteroom and the gatehouse, which also show a marked similarity to those at Kempley in Herefordshire and Elkstone in Gloucestershire. It has also been suggested that the bosses of St Augustine's daughter house at Keynsham also came from Bristol's Chapter House. The north and south walls are each divided into two bays, the upper sections of which are decorated with woven chevron and diaper (lozenge) patterns, which gradually merge into each other. Along the length of the north, south and west walls above the *sedilia* is a pattern of interlaced arcading, decorated on the north and south walls with a design of spirals with nailhead borders. Although spirals are by no means uncommon in Romanesque art across Europe, they may also, in England, be evidence of artistic continuity from the Anglo-Saxon period. The crypt at Repton, dating from the eighth century, is decorated in them, and they also survive on the drum-piers at Durham. In the Bayeaux Tapestry, a nailhead spiral column has been seen between Aelgyfa and the priest.

The rows of pointed arches on the north and south walls produced by the intersecting semi-circles of the arcading are outlined by these spirals, while the semi-circles themselves have a nailhead decoration. Each alternate supporting column is decorated with a spiral, while the capitals boast a variety of designs, many of which are elaborations of scalloped work. Such capitals are absent from all but the lower row of arcading on the west wall, possibly due to its awkward shape. The ninth column from the west on both the north and south walls, and the fourth from the west on the north, are identical to some of the columns in the gatehouse, which also supports the view that the latter was built at the same time as the Chapter House. The vault's ribs are supported by flat buttresses halfway along their length, with spiral columns supporting scalloped capitals either side of them. The arcading is underlined by a spiral string-course, with the *sedilia* beneath simply carved out of the ashlar and framed with simple roll-moulding supported by unor-namented jambs. The upper row of interlace arcading on the west wall, although similar, lacks the capitals and plinths on the other walls, possibly due to its awkward shape, though it still possesses chevron designs on the jambs and spirals over the arches. Similar arcading, also with contemporary capitals, appears on the west front of Malmesbury Abbey. Halfway down the central shaft above the door on the west wall, however, the spiralling changes direction, albeit temporarily, either due to an error during restoration by a later mason or as part of a deliberate scheme to emphasis this central point on the wall. The two windows either side of the doorway are set into decorated hood-moulds, the dripstones around medi-eval windows designed to divert dripping rainwater away from them, which rise up into the nailhead spiral string-course set above the door. The two subsidiary windows are set below the *tympanum*, the stone slab filling the gap between the arch and the doorway proper, itself placed beneath the roll-mouldings.

The walls and vault of the Chapter House were probably painted, as the remains of a red pigment and another, darker colour, were found during archaeological investigations carried out in the 1980s. Though the Chapter House at Bristol may have lacked the painted *Old* and *New Testament* scenes adorning that at Worcester, it may, like the latter, have had the backs of its *sedilia* painted in drapery designs. The room would also no doubt have also been furnished in its heyday with a lectern and crucifix.

Although now isolated some little distance away from the abbey under-neath the Central Library, the gatehouse was originally part of the great monastic complex. The upper parts of the gatehouse are perpendicular, probably built under the aegis of Abbot Newland, whose eponymous roll records that he was responsible for work on it. The lower parts, however, including the main vaulted gate and its companion Postern Gate, are both late Romanesque, remarkable for their lack of weathering. So remarkable, in fact, that it has been suggested that at some point after their construction they were subjected to major restoration, while one historian, noting the existence of mason's marks on some of the stones, even one which allegedly bore the date 1712, believed that the building may even have been taken apart, numbered, and then put back together again, in a manner similar to

**63** *The postern gate from the north, showing pillars, and chevron arch*

**64** *The postern gate from the south*

the methods used by some Victorian millionaires when moving some of their recently purchased palaces and monuments to other parts of the country, such as Bristol's former eighteenth-century bathhouse, which was taken to Port Meirion in Wales, and even to America. Although reconstruction work did occur in the nineteenth century, it made little impact on the Romanesque parts of the gatehouse, which shares features, such as the nailhead arcading, with the Chapter House.

The arch on the north side of the main gate is carved into three recessed sections. The first section is similar to the arcading on the west side of the Chapter House, in that the arches run directly into the jambs without intervening capitals, and also includes chevron ornamentation. The middle section is composed of nailhead bands interwoven with two plain, parallel bands. Its arch is supported by capitals decorated with flat palmettes, themselves supported on nailhead decorated jambs with spirals, another feature shared with the Chapter House. Within the gate itself is another quadripartite ribbed vault, divided into northern and southern bays. Although each rib is imitated in the adjacent bays, they are treated quite individually in the same bay. One of the northern ribs is plain, though flanked by the nailhead design. Its fellow is also decorated with the nailhead design, though has a double moulding. These same patterns are repeated on the southern bay, but on opposite ribs to those on the north. The chevron pattern runs around three sides of the transverse rib, with spines decorating its borders. The same motif recurs on a row of interlaced arches carved into the masonry under a spiralled string-course with a nailhead border. The arch on the south side of the gatehouse is divided

**65** *Romanesque door to abbey gardens, Bristol Cathedral*

into four recessed sections, decorated with chevrons and nailhead lozenges, the chevrons on its underside bordering a floral design. The zigzag pattern here is particularly elaborate and the use of capitals between the jambs and the arches is uninterrupted, perhaps indicating that this part of the building may have been carved by a different, perhaps later, generation of masons.

The postern gate on the west side of the main gate also shares the same elaborate decoration on its north side with a woven nailhead pattern on the outer section of the arch, but exceeds its companion in the richness of decoration on its capitals. Although comparatively plain compared to its neighbour, a sixteenth-century woodcut suggests it may at one time have boasted a vault and more elaborate decoration, while a blocked door in the west may have once opened onto a porter's lodge. The only obvious alteration to this part of the gateway is a flat Tudor arch, presumably added with the rest of the perpendicular structure built above the Romanesque. It is in their rich decoration on the gatehouse and Chapter House of the abbey of St Augustine that the sculptors of the late Romanesque so magnificently began to antici-pate the glories of the approaching Gothic.

Aside from these fine examples of the mason's craft, other fragments of the abbey's Romanesque structure still exist. These include three doorways just south of the Chapter House. Through one of these is a stairwell, leading up to the former dormitory, which contains fragments of the same chevron and lozenge patterns used to decorate the Chapter House and gatehouse. The second doorway, next to the stairwell, stands at the entrance to a small passage leading out to the abbey graveyard. Although this doorway is plain and unadorned, the cemetery archway, on the other hand, is decorated with three recessed stages and a little nailhead ornamentation. The third doorway, further south again, is decorated with half-shafts supporting a sub-arch resting on scalloped capitals.

Set into the south wall on the outside of the Chapter House, but originally from elsewhere in the abbey complex, is a fourth doorway, the flat arch of which is decorated by a chevron border cutting into a roll-moulding. Each peak of the zigzag is further decorated by a highly stylised floriate carving, while the overall impression of the door's decoration is that of a pre-beakhead style of ornamentation, with the teeth of the chevron as it covers the mouldings forming a kind of proto-beak protruding from the decorations' almost face-like shapes.

This part of the abbey grounds also contains a vaulted undercroft, three bays wide and two bays deep, measuring c.5m by 4m. As in the rest of the Romanesque building, the walls and vaulting are made of Brandon Hill Grit, while the supporting free-standing columns, whose capitals, like most of those in the main structure, are scalloped, and of ashlar masonry. Although the structure, which the undercroft supported, has since vanished, it has been suggested that this was once the calefactory, or warming room, where a fire was lit to warm the monks during the winter cold.

**66** *Bristol Bridge looking towards St Peter's*

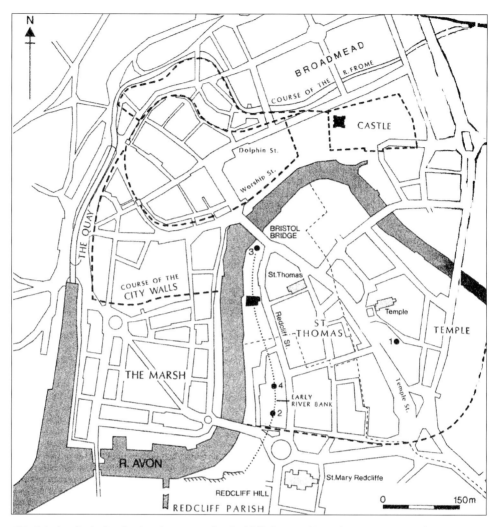

**67** *Bristol and suburbs, showing sites excavated at Redcliffe Street and Temple Fee.* Courtesy of Les Good

At the south-west corner of the monastic complex stands the Lower Gate, another important remnant of the abbey's former glory. This was formerly the gatehouse to the abbot's lodgings, and, like the abbey gatehouse, includes two arches constructed with the same stone and decoration as the Chapter House. The outer gate has plain jambs, scalloped capitals and an arch carved into three recessed stages. The outer recess has the same basketwork-like woven design as the small arch on the abbey gatehouse. The two inner recesses are decorated with the chevron, zigzag design, which, on the outer stage of the two is used to ornament a moulded spine carved around the arch's two faces. The whole is framed by a simple *bas-relief* zigzag border. The Lower Gate's eastern arch, although only possessing one recessed stage, shares the same basketwork pattern, plain jambs and scalloped capitals as its fellow. Fragments of an almost identical design survive at Brinsop in Herefordshire, while similar patterns emulating textiles can be found on the fonts at Castle Frome and Eardisley.

While certainly not as visible as the abbey complex above, the culvert revealed during archaeological investigation of the Cathedral School's playground in July 1987 was a no less necessary part of abbey life. This was found 5m below the main level of the playground, then the Lesser Cloister's south walk, 29.5in (75cm) wide, and extending eastwards for about 30m, where it had collapsed due to later disturbance. The 19.6in (50cm) thick drain walls, like the abbey itself, are constructed of Brandon Hill Grit and capped by 5.2in (16cm) thick slabs of Pennant Sandstone. A mix of mortars had been used throughout the drain's long history, though the earliest was the same red sandy mortar used in the construction of the town walls. It is probable that the drain was the main outlet for the abbey's *reredorter*, situated just east of the later medieval Lesser Cloister, also taking waste from the kitchens to the west, and the *frater*, the abbey's refectory, and *lavatorium*, the washroom, to the north. Access into the drain was gained through a manhole, built over a missing capstone, 2m west of one of the classrooms then under construction. The floor of the drain at the manhole was composed of a large stone block, cut into a shallow V-shaped section, possibly of lias limestone. Going eastwards from the manhole the height of the drain changed considerably, from 1.1m above a level of silt, 27.5in (70cm) deep to over 3m at one section 3m east of the manhole. This section was 5m long, possibly suggesting the existence here of a later *garderobe*. At the manhole, the drain's roof was tunnel-vaulted with a pointed arch, while at the putative *garderobe* it was supported by arches of pitched Pennant Sandstone with keystones of oolitic limestone. 14m east of the manhole, however, the drain's roof, now of horizontal capstones of the same type of rock, was reduced to only 31.4in (80cm) above the silt. As at the remains of the ditches at the City Castle, both sides of the drain's walls contained putlog holes 6.6in (17cm) square for the medieval timber scaffolding. Three small channels opened on to the north side of the drain, while on its south side were a similar set of three outlets. The water used to flush through the drain may have come from the conduit passing west of the lower Norman gate, the fishponds in the Abbot's Park south-west of the abbey, and the stream to the complex's south. A drainage system of similarly large dimensions was discovered in Bristol in the remains of the early thirteenth-century Franciscan Friary of Greyfriars at Lewin's Mead. Built at the same time as the drain's north wall, and set high up, were two small oolitic limestone gutters with a slightly larger companion further to the west. On the drain's southern wall were an additional three outlets, much larger than those to the north, with jambs and lintels of dressed oolite, which may have extended as far as Canon's Marsh, or perhaps even to the River Avon.

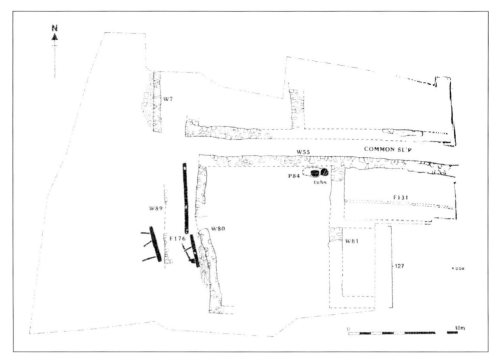

**68** *Plan of the Waterfront at Dundas Wharf in the mid- to late twelfth century.* Courtesy of Les Good

While the drain's west end is located 5m below the modern school play-ground, at the time of its construction this was probably the ground level underneath the low cliff on which the abbey was built, a position which would allow access to the drain for cleaning and maintenance and explain its large construction. The continued use of the drain as a soakaway right up to the nineteenth century and well into the twentieth for the school playground, its branching outlets and its continued maintenance and repointing through the centuries, all testify to the skill and foresight of the original masons. The abbey as a whole shows not only their decorative skill, but also their ingenuity and expertise in sanitation and civil engineering, despite the obvious scientific limitations of their age. It was these skills, which began to be increasingly used in reclamation projects and the construction of the City's docks as the century wore on, on which the City's mercantile wealth and pride partly rested and was displayed.

# 11 *Virtute et industria*: industrial architecture and the expansion of the docks

As a coastal port, much of Bristol's topography and history has been shaped by its need to harness its riverine environment for the transport and shipment of goods, and the drainage and reclamation of the surrounding wetlands to provide more territory for the expanding town. This wet environment has left its mark not only on the City's layout, but also on the names of its constituent parts, such as Canon's Marsh, and Marsh Street, leading to the area bounded by the Avon and Redcliffe in the west, and the manor of Billeswick to its east, historically simply termed 'the Marsh'. Analysis of the organic remains recovered from the earliest excavated layers of sites at Lewin's Mead have confirmed this view of the City's historic environment. At that time a little way outside the City itself, Lewin's Mead was mixture of marsh and open woodland, used primarily for pasturage, whose insect life was typical of those inhabiting wetlands. This is roughly similar to the findings from the medieval waterfront at Redcliffe. Though the sample for this latter dated from the thirteenth century, it is safe to assume that earlier centuries were just as damp and boggy. The earliest structures found at Lewin's Mead, stake holes for a hurdle or cattle fence and a possible stone boundary wall, give a clear indication of its agricultural use. Found with these were pits, one of which may well have served as a makeshift latrine.

Although the most spectacular of the medieval public works was the diversion of the Frome c.1240, the evidence from dendrochronological dating of timbers from Dundas Wharf has radically revised the dating of the City's expansion south-west into Redcliffe and the construction of the docks there. While the pottery finds at Dundas Wharf at the north of Redcliffe Street suggested the late twelfth or early thirteenth century, the dates obtained from the tree rings were considerably earlier. From these, the earliest structure, a post–pit, was built around 1123-33, around the beginning of the second quarter of the twelfth century rather than at the century's end. Some of the oak used may even have been considerably older. The last ring on one sample, no. 15, for example, dates from 1050, indicating that it was felled some time after 1060, while that of another, no. 28, similarly dates from 1066. This would suggest that the timber used might have come from considerably older, Saxon sources, unless the later rings had been obscured, distorted or otherwise

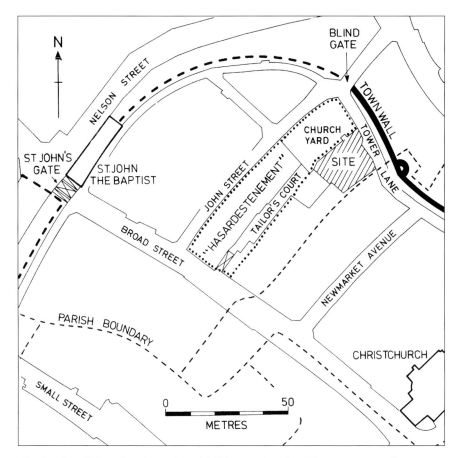

**69** *Location of Tower Lane house site and 1901 excavation of twelfth-century town wall.*
After E.J. Boore

failed to develop for some reason. Although green wood was commonly used in building work in the Middle Ages, especially in dock facilities where its use below the waterline meant there was no need to season it, several of the samples of wood taken from Dundas Wharf show signs of re-use from earlier, possibly more prestigious structures, so it is indeed quite possible that the wood in some of the early twelfth-century revetments may well have come from timber felled perhaps 60 years or so earlier. It now appears that the early twelfth century saw the construction of timber revetments along large sections of the Redcliffe riverbank, including not just Dundas Wharf but also at Bridge Parade and Redcliffe Street.

The riverfront at Redcliffe was some little distance further inland in the twelfth century than it is today, about 25-30m from the modern riverbank and approximately 20-25m from the middle of Redcliffe Street, which was probably intentionally built parallel to it. At the area in 93-95 Redcliffe Street the original riverbank was even closer to the modern street, only 15m away from its centre. Further south and west, on a line parallel with Redcliffe church, Redcliffe Hill terminated in a cliff stretching for 150m westwards from the Avon. At 93-95 Redcliffe Street the earliest form of reclamation appears to have commenced with the dumping of a layer of artificial clay over the riverfront's natural, alluvial clay, probably as a preventative measure against flooding by raising the land above the level of encroaching water. At the water's edge, the riverbank was held in place by a wicker revetment, a fence of hazel, oak and ash, supported by oak and birch posts sunk vertically. On the landward side, these may have formed part of a landing stage or similar structure. Although the remains of the revetment at Dundas Wharf are only fragmentary, at Bristol Bridge they survived to a height of 6m AOD. The earliest structures at Dundas Wharf appear to have been a post-pit dating from about the time of the last 12 years of the reign of Henry I. These wickerwork revetments were typical of other twelfth-century ports, such as Exeter and Norwich, with those of London and Wood Quay being particularly large. It is probable, however, that in their time they were only intended to be a temporary measure preceding the construction of stone quays. This began at Dundas Wharf around 1147 with the construction of river stairs and the associated stone quays, similar to those found at London.

These early docks at Bristol were double quays, like those at Hull, made necessary by the high tidal range at Bristol. Water levels may rise by between 4 and 13m during high tide, with a further difference of 3.3m during the spring and neap tides. These quays were split into two levels, the lower of which was a masonry platform on which a ship could rest, moored to the upper quay to prevent it from falling over during ebb tide when otherwise the fall in the water level would have left it below the quay. When, during the

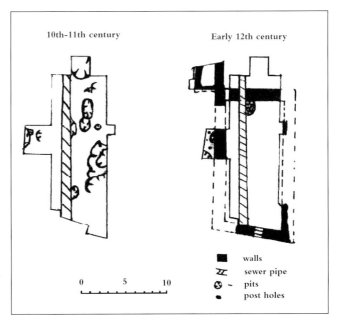

**70** *Saxon and Norman phases of the Tower Lane building.* After E. J. Boore

neap tide, there was insufficient water to reach the upper quay, this masonry platform would serve instead. At Dundas Wharf the earliest remains of these quays were two walls of Carboniferous Limestone, possibly quarried from the cliffs at the Avon gorge or Durdham Downs. The evidence from the quays at Dundas Wharf suggests that once the masonry walls were built, the spaces behind them were packed with domestic or industrial rubbish during low tide. Work ceased during high tide, when the river overflowed these walls to deposit layers of silt and clay. Two large timbers lay in front of the upper quay, held in place by small stakes and posts, with mortice holes for upright timbers cut into their upper sides. These were probably the base plates for a loading platform abutting the quay, which, if they were like the Thames waterfront in London, would also have had stairs. Later on in the century, when further riverfront walls replaced these quays, these timbers became part of a box-like structure with plank shutters at the sides, which may either have been a fish trap or a latrine, with the shutters opening out to allow the river water to flush away the detritus.

Leading down to the lower quay from Redcliffe Street was the 'Common Slip', a narrow cobbled lane for carts, one of a number of similar roadways constructed along the river's edge during the Middle Ages. At Canynges House the slip was stepped to provide private access to the river for the owners of the two adjacent properties. A stone jetty, probably for mooring small boats, extended into the river instead of a lower quay, a feature that was probably prohibited at the public docks unless the boats were much larger than those at Dundas Wharf.

This period also saw the construction of similar docks on the eastern waterfront of Bristol Bridge Parade, where excavation revealed a series of walls and stonework running from east to west and north to south. One of these might well have been the remains of an early riverfront, demolished during the first stages of the land reclamation, which was to extend the waterfront further out into the river. Set against the south side of one of these walls were a number of large wooden planks, probably part of a contemporary walkway or jetty, underneath which was found the possible remains of a timber tie-back running south from the riverfront nearly at a right angle. This was probably one of a series of riverfronts preceding the construction of the City's first stone bridge there in 1247. Further traces of a north to south running wall were found further south of this, along with traces of a possible wooden fence, and the remains of a wall, 22.4in (57cm) wide, and with a top level of 6.9m AOD, running for 4.8m eastwards underneath a cellar belonging to the keg store of the then Courage's Brewery. The walls on this section of the site, south of the future bridge, one of which possessed a short section of return walling aligned to one of the other walls, were frequently disturbed where the area had been used as the site for the slipway and associated reclamation projects of the late twelfth to early thirteenth centuries and the construction of tenements in the late thirteenth and early fourteenth centuries. Although these possessed floors of Pennant Sandstone resting on a layer of rough yellow sand, they were set against the mid-twelfth-century wall, showing where the wall had been incorporated into the later structure and where it may even have formed the footings for a tenement return wall set at right angles.

Whilst the area at Bridge Parade had to wait until the late thirteenth century for the construction of tenements, building began much earlier at 95–97 Redcliffe Street and Dundas Wharf. At 95–97 Redcliffe Street the rear wall of a building was found, which was at least 3.8m square. Although it is unclear what the building was used for, the lack of a hearth on the property suggests it may have been a workshop or warehouse. Found amongst the debris on its floor was a small soapstone mould, about 1.3in (3.5cm) long by 1.1in (2.8cm) wide at its largest end and 0.23in (6mm) thick, possibly for casting a small brooch shaped rather like a cogwheel. The house was rebuilt several times, during which the floor was raised by about 7.87in (20cm), probably as another measure against flooding. Contemporary with this building were three pits, possibly used for tanning. These would have been filled with a solution containing tannin derived from crushed oak bark in which the hides would be placed. The hides would have been soaked in successively stronger solutions of tannin until the process was complete and they could finally be passed on to a currier for dressing into finished leather. If these pits were used for tanning, it was only briefly. They were subsequently filled with clay, though the site still seems to have been used for industry as fragments of iron, and layers of cinder and charcoal over the clay suggest that it may have been part of a forge or iron foundry. A few burnt slabs dating from the earliest cinder layer were probably the remains of its hearth. Although the stone building remained the only building on the site, this later phase of occupation saw the construction of wooden fences marking out the boundaries of four properties, each 3.5m in width. This early stone house was demolished later in the twelfth century and moved slightly westwards and southwards a few centimetres, as further revetments were built to reclaim and stabilise the rapidly advancing waterfront.

Further evidence of industry on Redcliffe Street came from the remains of the original tenement plots for 127, 128 and 129 Redcliffe Street. These were the first buildings using stone foundations in this part of Redcliffe Street, though the natural alluvial soil of the marsh was marked with the pit- and postholes of sizable timber buildings erected at the time of the first quays, as well as possibly cranes and other dockside structures. Found with these were the remains of earlier stone walls, though it was impossible to discern any complete buildings or even their size or probable function, apart from the above tenements. 127 and 128 were probably built at the same time, as the same stretch of wall ran through both properties, serving as their end wall. This end of both tenements was rebuilt in 1182, suggesting that they were both owned by the same person at this date, or alternatively that it was done as a co-operative venture between neighbours. The front of these tenements was almost on the waterfront itself, with only a very small strip of land between them and the river. Number 129 in particular during its long history had a succession of side entrances leading from its interior to the Common Slip, the earliest of which was positioned so close to the wall of the upper quay that only a narrow section of it came before the front of the building itself.

At the back of 128 were found the remains of two wooden tubs, each 31.5in (80cm) in diameter, occupying a pit 31.5in (80cm) deep, with a 3.9in (10cm) thick deposit of lime in their bottoms. They were probably used for the first stages of the tanning process, where the cleaned hides were soaked in a mixture of lime, water and sometimes urine to break up the outer layers of skin and loosen the hair, preparatory to the next stage when the flesh and hair would be scraped away from the skins. These would then be soaked yet again, this time in a trypsin solution, derived from canine or avian faeces, to soften the skin and make it more receptive to the tanning solutions when it was finally immersed in the vats. The tubs' small size, however, suggests that rather than being used to treat cattle hides, they were instead used for tawing sheep or goat skins, a similar process to tanning but one in which the skins were treated with salt and alum, rather like the mordants used in the dye process. Unfortunately, none of the pits for the tanning process, like those associated with the stone building at 95–97 Redcliffe Street, were found either at 128, nor its neighbour 127, with which it may conceivably have shared a yard. It is possible that their remains had been destroyed or rendered unrecognisable by the centuries of subsequent building work which had disturbed much of the earlier remains at the site, or, perhaps less likely, that the workshop here was producing vellum and parchment rather than complete tanned leather. If this was the case, the hides were thus only being limed and scraped before being dried, ready for use as writing material.

The twelfth-century tanning or tawing tubs were probably housed in a small shed at the rear of the main building, which was divided into two rooms: a small one on the street front, behind which was a much larger room, while a passage ran past both of these to the rear of the premises. The small room was probably the business' shop or retail area, while the much larger room was most likely the workshop. The proprietor's living quarters were probably on the first floor, above the business section. This is if the pattern of occupation at 128 followed that of other contemporary *messuages*, though it is possible that the tanner and his family may have lived in privacy in the large, rear room on the ground floor. There was not enough material to indicate which part of the building served as its living quarters, though when the tenement was used as a dyeworks in the thirteenth century it is clear that these were indeed on the first floor, the ground floor given completely over to business with the larger room housing the dye vats.

The excavations at Bridge Parade uncovered 64 shards of pottery. The earliest pottery on the site was shards of the BPT 10 and 115 cooking pot fabrics. The other wares together were produced from 1120–1250, and it is likely that the majority of this later pottery, of whatever fabric, came from the decade around 1150 when the docks were under construction. Over three quarters of the pottery, 78 per cent, were storage jars and cooking pots. Fourty-eight per cent of the site's twelfth century pottery was Ham Green ware, including that of the commonest type of clay, BPT 32 and the coarser, proto-Ham Green fabric BPT 114. There were also five shards from three jugs in the early Ham Green A fabric, BPT 26, which was produced from 1120-70. One of these fragments was the handle and rim of a large jug or pitcher, the handle decorated with diamond rouletting, while inside the otherwise plain rim was a ledge, possibly to support a lid, while the exterior was glazed green. The precise form of the original jug is unknown, although it is possible that it was similar to a tripod pitcher with a similar rim, though lacking the internal ridge with a tubular spout, made of the pottery fabric BPT 18 c. Twenty-five per cent of the shards were made of a calcareous fabric tempered with flint from west Wiltshire, BPT 46, which was produced for a century from 1150-1250. These early pots showed that the site might have been occupied from the end of the eleventh century, unless the remains of such unfashionable pottery had been brought by the new settlers at Redcliffe when they moved into the area early in the twelfth century.

Outside of Redcliffe, possible remains of other wharves dating from the early twelfth century have been found at Lewin's Mead. Finds of early nails and roves associated with boat-building, and the whetstones necessary to sharpen the engineer's tools, suggest that a pit situated 17m inland from a small creek, lined with waterborne boulders and at least 1.6m below the contemporary riverbank, may have been the head of a very small boatyard or harbour. The pit and gully to the west of this pit may have originally been a small wharf, with the stub of wood found in another pit a possible mooring post. Later, when the great Norman hall came to be constructed nine metres or so further south, this was covered by a short slipway, though it is possible that this building still possessed some kind of quay. It is possible that the area could have been the site of a ferry across the Frome. The author of the *Gesta Stephani* describing the advice given to the king to dam up both the rivers during his 1138 siege, states that this was necessary as the Bristolians obtained their supplies by rowing boats. It may well be that the possible wharf or ferry site may have been one such supply route into the City. If boats were indeed being built at that site on the Frome, it may have been easier to launch them than in the City docks proper, as there the practice in the Middle Ages seems to have been to build them behind the timber revetments, which were then broken up to allow the ship to pass into the river. Although it is now considered that before its diversion the Frome, rather than running alongside Baldwin Street, was actually situated much further south, past Batten's Yard and Rackhay at the Marsh Wall, at the foot of the ramparts of the city walls between St Giles' Church and St Leonard's Gate next to the Frome ran Pyle Street, or '*le Pylle*', whose name suggests that the Frome was certainly navigable at this point, if only for the lighters and small rowing boats mentioned by Stephen's advisers. During the major engineering work of the mid-thirteenth century, quays for larger vessels were certainly constructed here.

Away from the City docks, excavations at Union Street in 2000 unearthed the remains of a large mercantile residence from the twelfth century. Then located just outside the city walls on land belonging to the Priory of St James', the house was built of yellow lias limestone. It possessed a garden on its northern side, while to its south was an industrial area, consisting of a cobbled courtyard with two pits, one circular, the other oval, both lined with stones. Beyond this courtyard was part of the medieval wall keeping in the Frome, which probably supplied the workshop's water. The proximity of a good water supply was undoubtedly an important factor in the location of many industries, such as the siting of the Redcliffe workshops along the waterfront, and their fellow at Union Street on the Frome. Although the precise industry carried out on the site is unknown, it is tempting to think they might have been dye or tanning pits, considering the development of the textile trade in the suburb further south. Underneath the house itself was further evidence of the site's early occupation as an industrial site in the remains of a circular furnace and stone hearth, though this would seem to suggest iron smelting and metalworking rather than textiles. Regardless of the precise industry practised at the site, its existence attests to the City's growing industrial strength and its involvement in the common trends of twelfth-century urbanisation. It was during this century that suburbs were founded as a means of isolating the noise, odours and nuisance of industry within a specialised area outside of the main residential core. Redcliffe, with its leather and dyeworks, was one such industrial suburb. The merchant's house in Union Street shows that a similar process of industrial expansion and isolation was also occurring in this area too. It was the start of a long tradition of manufacturing industry in this part of the City. Although principally given over to retail today, lined with shops, restaurants and with the Odeon cinema at its bottom, during the eighteenth and nineteenth centuries it was the site, amongst other things, of Fry's chocolate factory, the foundations of which disturbed part of the medieval remains.

Thus, Bristol in the early twelfth century saw the initial phases of the City's industrial and geographical expansion, physically embodied in the construction of the new harbour facilities, and industrial suburbs which would invigorate other areas of the City later in the thirteenth century and provide a sure foundation for the City's mercantile prosperity, particularly when this increasingly came to rest on the suburbs' cloth exports. It was this era, which saw Bristol become part of the general revival of urban life throughout Europe, and, through her trade and exports, become part of the wider European economy.

# 12 Design for living: domestic architecture

Apart from the City's great public works, the military, ecclesiastical and industrial building projects, which produced the churches, Castle, abbey and docks, many of Bristol's leading citizens were also willing and able to build their private homes in stone, fashionably decorated in the style of the contemporary Romanesque. Unfortunately, like the other buildings of the time with the exception of the Cathedral Chapter House, none of these have survived intact. Nevertheless, three domestic residences, clearly belonging to powerful individuals have been discovered in Tower Lane, Cyder House Passage and Lewin's Mead. With its western end facing Broad Street, the house in Tower Lane was large, 16m long by 7m wide internally, externally 18m by 9m, with 1.23 metre thick walls of Brandon Hill Millstone Grit, bonded with the same buff sandy mortar used on the western defences of the Castle and the Norman town walls. The footings on its southern wall were 1.2m deep, while the side walls' internal footings were 1.6m thick. The house's eastern end, angled obliquely towards the north to face the outside street or cliff directly, possessed an entrance with at least two oolitic limestone steps. Outside at the house's south-west corner was a *garderobe*, 3.5m by 1.5m by 1.4m internally, while inside the house at this corner was a stone hearth built somewhat later. In the south wall a coin from the reign of Henry I was found, while the foundations of the eastern wall yielded pottery of a similar date.

The house was similar to merchants' dwellings with undercrofts for storage of a slightly later date found at Southampton, with the Bristol building's own undercroft partly below the then ground level. Although subsequent building activity had removed all the evidence of its original occupation, it is possible that the building had been constructed by FitzHarding himself. He is known to have built a house in Broad Street during the century, and, despite being the town's reeve, was probably of bourgeois rather than aristocratic origins, similar to the wealthy merchants at Southampton.

Another twelfth-century building was discovered off Broad Street in 1990, at Cyder House Passage. Unlike the Tower Lane house to its north, this had its longest sides running from north to south, rather than east to west, and was 12m long by 5.5m wide internally, and externally 14m long by 7m wide. Its northern gable had become part of the boundary wall separating the parishes of Christchurch and St John, and the other tenements to the house's north, including the Tower Lane house. This gable end, like the *domus conversorum* at Dolphin Street, had also possessed at least one undercroft window in its time.

Outshining this, however, is the late Romanesque building excavated at Lewin's Mead. This building, angled north-west to south-east, with sides 17m long, was not quite square as its south-eastern end is believed to have been a metre longer, and the northwestern end was not straight. The level of the original undercroft floor was probably under 5.7 to 6m OD, 3m below modern ground level. The first of its walls to be built was probably the north-eastern, whose bottom course of footings was below 5m OD. These supported walls 1.4m thick, though one of these narrowed by 11.8in (30cm) in two stages. These walls had, in places, survived to a height of 8.3 and 8.45m OD. The walls were mostly constructed of Brandon Hill Grit with a mixture of carboniferous and oolitic limestone, and Pennant Sandstone, bonded with the reddish-brown sandy mortar, roughly similar to the construction of the other great Norman buildings in Bristol. The wall was supported by a buttress at its extreme north-eastern corner to guard against subsidence in the boggy soil. It was a wise precaution, as during the intervening centuries the walls had fallen away from the vertical in two places by about 4 and 6 degrees respectively. 2m from the end of the north-eastern wall was a doorway, 1.45m wide, with oolitic jambs 1.7m tall, the external sides of which had been chamfered. The mortar used to bond them was of white lime. The door hinges' lower pintles still survived on both jambs. It is believed that if the door's arch had been round, then the door might have been 2.4m high. Leading down into the building were five steps, each composed of several slabs of Brandon Hill Grit, and bonded with a red-light brown clay on their south sides and light brown soil on their north, with no apparent reason for this change of mortar. The lowest step was set 7in (18cm) into the building's west wall. Below these were the footings of the door itself, projecting a quarter of a metre into the room to strengthen the door. The floor of the building was probably 6.2m OD. Constructed rather later, but still as an integral structure to the eastern wall, the northern wall varied between 5.4 and 5.7m OD along the eastern wall. Surviving to the same height as its neighbour, its own foundations were 1.2m thick. Its footings were 5.8 to 9.8in (15 to 25cm) wider than the wall itself, increasing to 17.7in (45cm) to strengthen it where it joined the eastern wall. Finds of horizontal timbers suggested that piles or a wooden raft partially supported the wall, a necessary measure as it may well have been built over backfilled material. It was an engineering technique used elsewhere in the city to counteract possible subsidence caused by the marshy soil. Further afield, Salisbury Cathedral is supported entirely by one such raft. The central section of the Lewin's Mead building's northern wall had been robbed out, but a section had survived at the western corner. This had been built on top of pieces of Brandon Hill Millstone Grit the size of a human fist in a foundation trench between 1.3 and 2.1m wide, rather than being supported by the wooden piles further east. The wall's three tiers of footings extended the wall by another 1.15m. The fragments of Brandon Hill grit reached up to the first tier of the footings, above which was a mixture of natural red and blue-grey clay, mixed with lime, stones and wood. This corner had a buttress, similar to that on the eastern corner, 35.4in (90cm) wide. The western wall was bonded to the northern wall and shared its construction. The remains of the southern porch lay 17m away from the northern wall. The entrance was 2.08m wide. From the evidence of the surviving bases it appears the height of the floor was approximately 8.9m OD. Although now elliptical, with the underside of the arch now 2.6m above the level of the floor, the original doorway was probably 11.8in (30cm) higher, so that the porch was 2.9m from top to bottom. A hawk's-bill dripstone with a narrow, flat separating band and a probable foliate stop began the building's mouldings. The arch was simply decorated, its main moulding consisting of a large roll emerging from the upper part of the capital supporting the architrave. The capital's vertical face was chamfered with a lightly incised line. A fragment of the original decoration, a volute carved into leaves whose upper parts end as bunches of fruit survived on the western capital, while the eastern capital possessed two bunches of three stems each, which each rose up into simple, three-lobed leaves. A larger plantain leaf appears to have decorated the capital's south-eastern corner, but has since become broken off. A hollow, designed to hold water, supported by a vertical capital chamfered out to a lower base formed the end of its circular shaft. The moulding's underside was supported by a similar base.

This building was divided by two, not quite parallel arcades of three piers each running its length, dividing it into three aisles, each arcade consisting of four bays. The central bays were 3.5m wide while those flanking it were 4m wide. The parts of the building excavated were probably its undercroft, whose lack of stone vaulting suggests its first floor was probably built of suspended timbers. Originally the undercroft's arcading's piers extended to this timber ceiling, which they may have partially supported by the offset courses set into some of their lower stages, bearing columns which extended beyond this into the second floor, dividing that into aisles in turn. The level of the south door corroborates this view, as well as suggesting that the headroom in the under-croft was probably 2.9m. At the time of the excavation, two columns were still standing, and there were remnants of three of the piers, plus evidence of a fourth, which had been considerably rebuilt somewhat later. The sixth pier and three of the half-columns or piers attached to the wall had been robbed out, while the original arches had also been removed during later rebuilding work. Their original shape is not known, though it is likely that they were round like the doorway arch. Probably typical of the construction of all the building's piers was that of the south arcade's east column, despite this column having been removed at a later date. This pier was composed of a Pennant Sandstone and Brandon Hill Grit core, bonded with red sandy mortar, surrounded by dressed oolite blocks. The pier's base rested at a depth of 5.64m OD on a layer of gravel stones of Brandon Hill Grit the size of a fist. It had

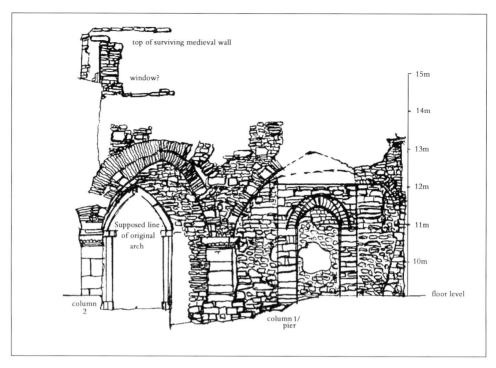

**71** *Romanesque arcade and later features at building at Lewin's Mead.* After R. Price and M. Ponsford

originally been square, but the south face had later been removed during further building work. The first course of masonry at the pier's base was 1.34m wide, 7in (18cm) high, with a 60 degree chamfer where it joined the main body of the base. The top of the pier was 7in (18cm) below the top of the south-western column at 8.57m, indicating that one course of masonry had been robbed.

The westernmost column of the south arcade was carved from oolitic, probably Dundry, limestone, and bonded in white lime mortar. The supporting pier was composed of two stages, together 1.24m square by 8.75m OD high. It supported two courses of masonry collectively 11.8in (30cm) in height and 1 metre square, upon which rested a pedestal carved from a single freestone block 25in (64cm) wide, square at the base but rounded further up. This supported a shaft composed of four round drums, each 22.8in (58cm) in diameter, capped with a damaged square scalloped cushion capital 36.6in (93cm) wide. The capital's upper part was 11m OD. The undercroft's south-western andnorth-eastern piers were similar in construction, as was the south arcade's central column, whose round drums were the same diameter, with a similar square capital, though this had its upper portion at 10.94m OD. Indeed, the north-eastern pier's plinth was identical to its counterpart in the building's south-west. The southern arcade's central column had survived to the level of the upper part of its capital, despite burning and damage to its east side by later activity at the wall into which it had become embedded. At some time in its history it had been cut almost flush with the wall. Despite its similarity of decoration, it differed from its neighbouring column by not possessing a supporting pier.

The structure of the north-eastern pier, originally the same as the south-eastern and western piers, was partly obscured by the extensive reconstruction it had suffered on its southern side. The lower part of its base, 1.26m square, was twisted towards the north-east, while its bottom was 3.9 to 7.87in (10-20cm) wider than that of the south-western column. It similarly rested on foundations of clay and Brandon Hill Grit. The sites of the north arcade's central and western piers had been robbed, though investigation of the site of the fifth column suggested that its pier was similarly square. No further excavation of the site of the sixth pier was possible, as the robbing of the site for a cellar during the eighteenth or nineteenth centuries had made it inaccessible. A substantial fragment of the capital of one of the demolished columns, reworked by a later mason for reuse, was also found, while directly on the northern side of the northern arcade's central pier, sharing its gravel and Brandon Hill Grit foundations, was a series of flat slabs of Pennant Sandstone lying at 5.86m OD. These were almost certainly remnants of the building's original floor.

Although stone undercrofts had become a standard architectural feature of Norman first-floor halls since the middle of the twelfth century, the building at Lewin's Mead differed from most other halls of this type through its possession of aisles on the ground floor. These usually only occurred in Norman halls of one, ground floor only, or else were confined to the top floor of a first-floor hall, as in the Norman halls at Boothby Pagnall, the two-aisled building at Agnes Old Hall in Yorkshire, and Moyses Hall in Bury St Edmunds. One of the courses of masonry in the external walls would have been offset to take the floor's joists, though none were actually found, possibly due to them having been removed during the building's extensive reconstruction during the fourteenth century. No evidence was found of a window in the undercroft, though much of the external wall in which they would have been placed either had not survived or was inaccessible. If they existed, they would have been below ground level. Alternatively, the undercroft never in fact possessed any, being lit entirely by artificial lighting, such as that of a stone lamp recovered during the investigation.

A staircase led from the undercroft to the first floor, possibly wooden and built around the central column of the south aisle, as this lacked the square pier of the other columns. Another stairway may have been situated close by the east door for convenience. No trace of either stairway was found, though it is possible that if they were indeed wooden they would not have been attached to the columns but to the flooring, thus leaving no mark on the masonry. No trace of a hearth was found either, though there were traces of charcoal suggesting one existed. It may, if it existed, have been located between the trenches dug by the investigating archaeologists. The construction of a wooden first floor suggests that the undercroft may have been used for storage, like those of the merchants' houses at Southampton. If this were the case, there simply would have been no need for heating at that level. The location of the hall's kitchens and other outbuildings are similarly unknown, though it is possible that they were located in a much smaller building 11m to the north, though this is considered to date from a possibly later period.

With a width of 17m, the building at Lewin's Mead was only 15.78in (40cm) narrower than the largest Norman hall yet discovered, the house in Cuckoo Lane, Southampton, which was a massive 32.3m in length. Bristol Castle's own hall at 32.5m long by 16.2m wide was of similar dimensions, while an additional building, probably located on the hall's west side, and, like the building at Lewin's Mead, constructed of two stories, was 15.3m long by 8.1m wide. This latter served as the king's chambers when he was resident at the Castle. The similarity of the building's dimensions suggests, at the least, a certain uniformity in units of measurement, though these probably would not have been based on the widths of tenements, which were then still developing.

About 5m from the house itself was a pavement of pennant slabs laid on a mixture of grey-brown clay and organic material. Approximately 2m east of this, leading southwards down to the creek by which the house had been built, was a wooden platform or slipway. This consisted of two supporting walls of Brandon Hill Grit mortared with red clay, 5.9in (15cm) high and 15.7 to 19.6in (40-50cm) apart, laid across a layer of clay mixed with dark-brown soil. Resting on these walls was a pathway of oak planks. From a beginning height of 7.2m OD, they sloped down to the creek at an angle of approximately 25 degrees. It is also possible that the eastern doorway led out to a quay. The existence of the stone steps here demonstrates that the builders found it necessary to keep the external ground level above 7m OD to prevent flooding, as the undercroft's internal floors were some 19.6in (50cm) below the level of the medieval mean high tide. Unlike the other buildings found at the site, the hall appears to have been aligned towards the cliff edge towards its north–west, rather than the river, an economical use of space, which nevertheless left the hall potentially vulnerable to attack. Whoever owned the hall obviously felt sufficiently secure not to expect an assault.

The building's demolition in the fourteenth century means that the building's height is unknown, though from the undercroft's floor to the apex of the arch it probably measured between 6.4 and 6.7m. If the hall were primarily religious in purpose, as suggested by Worcester in the fifteenth century, who believed that it had been a priory of canons before the foundation of the hospital, then it would have had a clerestory, which would have raised the roof still further. These were unknown in secular aisled halls. Possibly it was roofed with shingles, although fragments of slate, possibly

Cornish, were found in the foundation trench. Regardless of the roof's precise form, it would have been braced by large trusses stretching from one external wall to another across each bay and supported by the arcading in each aisle.

As to the identity of its builder, although there is no documentary evidence for the building, let alone its owner from that date, the hospital that superseded it was founded by John de la Warre sometime between 1232-4, suggesting that the family already occupied the site by that time. Finds of pottery dating from c.1175 found amongst the backfilled material in the north wall's foundation trench suggest the building may therefore have been built by Jordan de la Warre I, his brother David I, or indeed David's son, John I, who were active at this time. The origins of the de la Warre family are obscure, though it is possible they were related to the FitzHardings. It has been claimed that Robert FitzHarding's two nephews, Jordan and David, were the two dynasts of the de la Warres mentioned above. Although *Warre* meant 'Warrior' in Anglo-Norman, one of Robert FitzHarding's sons was known as Robert de Were, from the estate of Weare near Axbridge in Somerset. It is possible that Warre was an alternative form of Were, possibly deliberately changed from a simple place name to something much more martial as an attempt to sound more impressive. If that is the case, then the precise relationship to the FitzHarding's is still unclear, as Jordan and David were clearly far too old when Jordan first appears in history, witnessing three charters dating from 1150-66, to be FitzHarding's grandsons. Nevertheless, some kind of relationship does seem to have existed as they were certainly witnesses to their charters, particularly one of 1164-70 in which Robert FitzHarding confirmed the liberties of those living on his lands, and in 1230 David de la Warre II owned Robert FitzHarding's former house in the City. A charter dated between 1148-83 refers to Jordan de la Warre holding land in Bristol in the area of Lewin's Mead, beyond the Frome on the road to the manor of Billeswick, which seems to corroborate the suggestion that the building may have been built by them. Its position next to a creek also reinforces this identification, as by the third quarter of the twelfth century the de la Warres appear to have had strong shipping interests. Jordan and David were paid by Henry II in 1172 for the hire of their ship and provisions for the conquest of Ireland, which may have included the siege engines and military equipment recorded elsewhere as having been shipped from Bristol. Like the other Bristolian mercantile families with extensive shipping interests, it is highly likely that the de la Warres possessed their own private quays, such as those at Canynge's House in Redcliffe. The small lighters and rowing boats used at the Frome would have ferried goods from ship to shore and from dock to dock.

Among the items found on the site was a stylus and child's leather boot, perhaps the property of the families working on the site. Also found in the north wall's foundation trench were the remains of hazelnuts, possibly part of the builders' meals during its construction.

By the thirteenth century the marshy ground on which the hall had been built had led to serious subsidence, especially at the east end. There is, unfortunately, no evidence for the hall's fate between its construction and the foundation of the hospital. Although it is assumed that the hall continued in use without major alteration after its completion, at the early stages of the excavation it was believed that the hall became perilously unsafe, even prone to collapse. This necessitated the bracing of the pillars by internal walls. The east wall was then demolished and the building filled with rubbish to bring the ground level roughly up to that of today. The building was extended eastwards, with the eastern porch built to lead into the southern aisle of the new building. Thus the hall was converted from private, secular use, to become the thirteenth-century hospital's chapel.

Although the building is Plantagenet, rather than strictly Norman, it was nevertheless built according to the conventions of the architecture they had spread and developed, if not actually introduced. As such, the hall represents one of the last, glorious flourishing of the late Romanesque in Bristol, before being overtaken by the triumphant Gothic.

## Postscript: the Plantagenets and beyond

The coronation of Henry Plantagenet as king of England marked the end of the Norman dynasty, and their replacement by one with their origins in Anjou, long antagonistic to the Normans. His ascent to the throne united in his person realms and fiefs as diverse as Aquitaine, inherited through his wife, Eleanor, Maine, Brittany, and Touraine, as well as his own patrimony of Anjou and Normandy, an area, though not then styled an empire, which stretched across the western seaboard of France, an area greater than the personal demesne of its Capetian kings. As a result, England became more firmly drawn into France's orbit, politically, economically and culturally, and from thence on to the wider European scene. The first few years of Henry's reign coincided with the pontificate of Nicholas Breakspear, who, as Adrian IV, was the first and only English pope. English nobles like William the Marshal competed in French tournaments for the prizes of chivalry, while clerks such as Thomas à Becket studied and taught at the university of Paris, and held benefices even further afield. John of Salisbury, the greatest Latin scholar of his age and a former pupil of Peter Abelard, became Bishop of Chartres. In the other conquered Norman kingdom, Sicily, an Englishman, Master Thomas Brown, had become secretary of King Roger II. Although recalled to England to supervise the exchequer, his career demonstrates the new, cosmopolitan world in which twelfth-century Englishmen lived and moved. To the medieval Chronicler William FitzStephen, the '*multe riche cite*' of London was the most famous city in the world, the wealthiest city in Christendom. And London was by no means alone in exploiting the commercial opportunities offered by the Angevin dominions.

Henry's charter of 1155 gave Bristolian merchants freedom from customs, passage and toll throughout England, Normandy and Wales, while excluding direct foreign competition in hides, corn and wool. This was probably to counter possible economic rivalry from Wales, as these were the main goods involved in trade with the principalities. The union with Aquitaine meant that the door was open for Bristolian merchants to become prominent in dealing with Bordeaux and Bayonne. By the mid-fifteenth century Bristol was the main port for the Gascon trade, responsible for half of all English cloth exports to the region. Bristol swiftly became the chief importer of Gascon wine, particularly claret. In succeeding centuries, the focus of this trade moved still further south, until by Henry VII's reign Bristol was the leading centre for trade with Spain and Portugal. The trading link with Ireland remained strong. Finds of Ham Green and Redcliffe ware in Ireland, particularly in Dublin, Cork and Waterford in the case of the former, show the importance of Irish trade, at least in the export of this commodity. Indeed, it was strengthened after the Angevin succession. According to the *Song of Dermot and the Earl*, Dermot gained Henry's aid through the personal intervention of Robert FitzHarding, then a very old man. Henry II, in return for Bristol's support of his invasion of 1171, gave Bristolians special privileges in Dublin. Dublin was given the liberties and customs of Bristol, which were in turn modelled on those of Breteuil in France. Of the new settlers in the city, many bore the surname *'de Bristou'*. This influence remained strong, despite the commercial rivalry of Liverpool and Chester, which changed Bristol's commercial links to the central and southern parts, notably Galway, Cork, Limerick, Ross, Kinsale and Waterford. Furthermore, under John, Bristol Castle became the headquarters of the Angevin forces in Ireland. Although England's foreign links now were to the south rather than the north, the Norse connection was never severed. Brian Borumha's victory over the Vikings at the Battle of Clontarf in 1014 did not expel them. It merely secured Brian as their overlord and high king. The Ostmen themselves survived. They were there in the persons of the Norse merchants of Dublin who came out to greet Henry II when he marched on the city during his invasion. There was a price to pay for such commercial and military expansion. While some Irish historians, such as Fr. F.X. Martin, have lamented the squandered opportunities presented by Henry's invasion for Ireland to have become an integral part of the new continental economy, one of the more obvious political effects of the invasion has been an intermittent cycle of 800 years of violence and recrimination, which has not yet been entirely broken in the twenty-first century. In central government, Henry II's court kept in touch with the Swedish and Norwegian monarchs. Direct trade with the north appears to have been slow to develop, however. The first reference to Bristolians sailing to Iceland is from 1424. It is possible, however that the trade had developed nine years previously. Nevertheless, the trade had its impact on local mercantile politics. One of those involved in the Icelandic trade was the younger William Canynges, whose father had sponsored the rebuilding of Redcliffe church. The Iceland trade was, however, probably an expansion of the Irish trade, resulting in a strange reversal of roles. Once Norse ships had come to Bristol by way of Dublin. Now Bristolians were finding their way to the former Norse colony by the same route. It was this expansion of the trade to Ireland, which gave Bristolian seamen the seafaring experience that gave Bristol a leading role in the discovery and the colonization of Newfoundland and New England. Even here there was a personal continuity with the city's leading burgesses of the twelfth century. The state of Delaware takes its name from Thomas de la Warre, governor of Virginia, and a scion of the same family that founded St Bartholomew's Hospital in the thirteenth century, and had witnessed FitzHarding's charters in the twelfth.

The first suburbs of Bristol were at Redcliffe and Bedminster, areas already in Bristol's orbit in the twelfth century, though the reclamation of St Augustine's and later St Philip's Marsh provided more space to assuage some of the land hunger afflicting a rapidly growing town. There was probably already some urban development of the Marsh during the Norman period. Another charter of Henry's, dating to 1165, mentions 'my men who dwell in my stead in the Marsh'. It is unlikely that a suburb sufficiently important to warrant royal attention could spring up within the short space of ten years. Redcliffe was important in the dyeing and local leather working industry from the thirteenth century onwards, trades already dating back to before the Conquest in the city. It was only in the fourteenth century, though, that Bristol began to export cloth on a major scale. When it came, the expansion was rapid. By 1365 Bristol was shipping 40 per cent of English cloth exports, though this was to decline to 15 per cent in the fifteenth century. The fair granted to the monks of St James attracted merchants from all over the country. Bristol owed much to its position on the Severn. Before the thirteenth century ships seem mostly to have rested on the alluvial mud around Bristol. Rapid silting of the waterfront at Redcliffe allowed the greater reclamation of land, but pushed shipping further west as they sought a suitable harbour. Further improvements to the port were made through the diversion of the Frome through St Augustine's Marsh, and the building of quays there, as well as the construction of the city wall enclosing this new urban expanse in the 1240s. More quays were established in Redcliffe, Broad Quay and Welsh Back. Broad Quay itself became the centre of Bristol's harbour until the construction of the docks at Avonmouth in the nineteenth century. With shipping went shipbuilding, an industry begun in medieval Bristol at Narrow Quay. These developments had to wait for the twelfth century, though. For the eleventh, Bristol remained confined to its narrow promontory between the Frome and Avon.

To its citizens, Bristol was always a city of churches. Succeeding generations continued the spate of church building begun by the Normans, so that by the end of the Middle Ages about 61 churches, chapels, convents and hospitals had been built in Bristol and its immediate environs to serve the spiritual, and sometimes physical needs of its citizens, not counting the 11 almshouses founded between the mid-thirteenth and sixteenth centuries. The Norman influence is most noticeable in the establishment of the town's monastic foundations. Of the eight houses established between the foundation of St James' Priory in 1137 and the Augustinian Friary in 1313, at least three were founded by Norman lords and ladies. Robert Fitzharding and his wife, Eva, were responsible for at least two, and the surname of the founder of the Dominican Blackfriars Friary, established by one Maurice de Gaunt or Berkeley. If the latter is his real surname, suggests that their dynasty may well have been responsible for a third also. It would certainly not be impossible. The same Maurice de Berkeley has been credited, along with several others, with the foundation of St John the Baptist and St Mark's, or Gaunt's, hospitals, while his kinsmen Robert and Thomas may have founded St Katherine's and St Mary Magdalene's. Just as Henry II had patronized the abbey, so his younger son also endowed charitable institutions within the city. King John· himself founded the leper hospital of St Lawrence when Earl of Mortain, and might also have founded, or at least patronized, that of St John the Baptist too.

It is possible to overestimate Bristol's importance, however. It only became a county in its own right in 1373. Before then, it was over-shadowed by the other, more ancient towns in the region, such as Bath and particularly Gloucester. Gloucester was the seat of county government, and after the dismantlement of the see of Worcester, the seat of ecclesiastical authority as well. Throughout the Anglo-Saxon period, Bristol had been part of the diocese of Worcester. Only after the Reformation did Bristol itself become a bishopric. Even during its commercial heyday in the fourteenth and fifteenth centuries the town was rivaled in size and prosperity by York and Norwich. Nevertheless, by the end of the thirteenth century Bristol's new bridge was on a par with the other large European cities, an equal of London and Paris. This was after the major engineering work of the 1240s, which more than doubled the city's area. This, however, was the culmination of a process of civic expansion begun more than a century earlier by the Normans, who in their turn built on the City's Saxon foundations. Although the City is no longer quite the industrial dynamo it was in the Middle Ages, modern Bristolians can trace their city's prosperity back over 900 years to when the early medieval city played a key role in determining the affairs of the kingdom, a time when it truly was 'almost the richest city.'

# Bibliography

## Sources in translation

Bede, *A History of the English Church and People*, trans. Shirley-Price, L., revised edition Latham, R.E., Penguin Books, 1968.

Bennett, J.A.W., and Smithers, G.V., eds, *Early Middle English Verse and Prose*, OUP, 1974

Garmonsway, G. N., ed. and trans. *The Anglo-Saxon Chronicle*, J. M. Dent 1972, *Holy Bible, New International Version*, Hodder and Stoughton, 1980.

Moore, J.S., ed. and trans. *The Domesday Book*, Vol.15, *Gloucestershire*, Phillimore Books, 1982.

Morgan, P., ed. The Domesday Book, Vol.1, Phillimore Books, 1983.

Riley, H.T., *The Annals of Roger de Hoveden comprising the History of England and of Other Countries of Europe*, Vol.1, Llanerch 1994.

Stevenson, J., trans. *Simeon of Durham: A History of the Kings of England*, Llanerch, 1987.

Stevenson, J., ed. and trans. *The History of William of Newburgh*, Llanerch, 1996. Swanton, M.J., *Anglo-Saxon Prose*, J.M. Dent, 1993.

Stevenson, J., ed. and trans. *The Chronicle of Florence of Worcester with a Continuation and Appendix*, Llanerch, 1996.

Stevenson, J., *The Hexham Historians and the Chronicle of Jordan Fantosme*, Llanerch, 2000.

Thorn, C. and J., eds, *The Domesday Book*, Vol. 8, *Somerset*, Phillimorem Books, 1980.

William of Malmesbury, and Peile, J.H.F. trans. *Life of Saint Wulstan, Bishop of Worcester*, Llanerch, 1996.

## Modern works

Alderson, L., *Rare Breeds*, Shire Publications Ltd, 1989

Allen, K., ed. *Domesday: 900 Years of England's Norman Heritage*, Millbank Publications and The National Committee for the 900th Anniversary of the Domesday Book, 1986.

Aston, M., and Bond, J., *The Landscape of Towns*, Sutton Publishing, 2000.

Aston, M., and Iles, R., *The Archaeology of Avon - A Review from the Neolithic to the Middle Ages*, Avon County Council, undated.

*Archaeology in Bristol 1988-1989*, Bristol and Avon Archaeology, Vol.7, 1988, p.33.

*The "Cweorn Cleofu" of the Pucklechurch Saxon Charter: an Unsolved Problem*.
BARG Bulletin, Vol.1, no. 1, Spring 1962, p.3.

Backhouse, J., Turner, D. H., and Webster, L., eds, *The Golden Age of Anglo-Saxon Art*, British Museum Publications, 1984.

Barlow, F., *The Feudal Kingdom of England 1042 - 1216*, Longman, 1988.

Barrett, W., *The History and Antiquities of the City of Bristol*, Alan Sutton, 1982.

Belsey, P., and Ponsford, M.W., *A Late Roman Buckle and Medieval Building at Stockwood*, in Bristol and Avon Archaeology 1, 1982, p.2-6.

Bettey, J.C., *St Augustine's Abbey, Bristol*, The Bristol Branch of the Historical Association Local History Pamphlets, 1996.

Bettey, Dr J.H., *St Augustine's Abbey*, in Rogan, Canon J., ed. *Bristol Cathedral: History and Architecture*, Tempus, 2000, p.15-37.

Boore, E.J., *Excavations at Tower Lane, Bristol*, Bristol Archaeological Research Group Bulletin Vol.6, no.7, April 1979, p.202.

Boore, E.J., A Summary Report of Excavations at Tower Lane, Bristol 1979-80, Bristol Archaeological Research Group Review, no. 1, 1980, p.18-26.

Boore, E.J., *Excavations at Peter Street, Bristol 1975-6*, Bristol and Avon Archaeology 1982, p.7-11.

Boore, E.J., *Excavations at Tower Lane, Bristol*, City of Bristol Museum and Art Gallery, 1984.

Boore, E.J., *Excavations at St Augustine the Less, Bristol, 1983-84*, Bristol and Avon Archaeology 4, 1985, p.21-33.

Boore, E.J., *The Church of St Augustine the Less, Bristol: An Interim Statement*, Transactions Bristol and Gloucestershire Archaeological Society, Vol.104, 1986, p.211-14.

Boore, E.J., *The Lesser Cloister and a Medieval Drain at St Augustine's Abbey, Bristol*, in Bristol and Avon Archaeology 6, 1987, p.31-4.

Boore, E.J., and Good, L., *St Peter's, Bristol, 1975*, in AGBA Report, Bristol Archaeological Research Group Bulletin vol.5, no.7, Spring 1976, p.191-2.

*Bristol Excavations 1975*, Bristol Archaeological Research Group Bulletin vol.5, no.5, Autumn 1975.

Burrough, T.H.B., *Bristol*, Studio Vista, 1970.

Caffall, W.A., *Thornbury – A Study in Local History: Part 1 – Domesday to 1300*, The Thornbury Society, undated.

Campbell, J., ed. *The Anglo-Saxons*, Penguin Books, 1982.

Cassady, R.F., *The Norman Achievement*, Sidgwick and Jackson, 1986.

Charlton, J., and Milton, D.M., *Redland 791 to 1800*, J.W. Arrowsmith, 1951.

Chibnall, M., *Anglo-Norman England 1066-1166*, Basil Blackwell, 1986.

Clanchy, M.T., *England and its Rulers 1066-1272*, Fontana, 1983.

Cox, S., *Excavations on the Medieval Waterfront at Bridge Parade, Bristol, 1999*, Bristol and Avon Archaeology, Vol.15, 1998, p.1-20.

Davey, C., *West Country Place-Names And What They Mean*, Abson Books, 1983.

Davis, R.H.C., *King Stephen*, Longman, 1990.

Dawson, D., *Archaeology and the Medieval Churches of Bristol, Abbots Leigh and Whitchurch*, Bristol Archaeological Research Group Review 2, 1981, p.9-26.

Deansley, M., *The Pre-Conquest Church in England*, Alan and Charles Black, London, 1961.

Dickinson, J.C., *The Origins of St Augustine's, Bristol*, in McGrath, P., and Cannon, J., eds, Essays in Bristol and Gloucestershire History, Bristol and Gloucestershire Archaeological Society, 1976, p.109-126.

Dixon, N., *An Archaeological Bibliography of Bristol*, Bristol Museum and Art Gallery, 1987.

Douglas, D., *Bristol under the Normans*, in McGrath, P., and Cannon, J., eds, Essays in Bristol and Gloucestershire History, Bristol and Gloucestershire Archaeological Society, 1976, p.101-108.

Everett, S., *A Reinterpretation of the Anglo-Saxon Survey of Stoke Bishop*, Transactions of the Bristol and Gloucestershire Archaeological Society, Vol.80, 1961, p.175-178.

*Excavations at St James' Priory, Bristol*, in Bulletin of the Bristol and Avon Archaeological Society no.15, Spring-Autumn 1995, p.4.

*Excavations at Union Street, Bristol*, Bristol and Avon Archaeological Society Bulletin no.28, Autumn 2000-Spring 2001, p.4.

Falkus, M., and Gillingham, J., *Historical Atlas of Britain*, Kingfisher, 1987.

Finberg, H. P. R., *The Formation of England 550 - 1042*, Paladin, 1974.

Fleming, P., *The Church and Parish of All Saints, Bristol: A History*, Diocese of Bristol Board of Education, 1999.

Fowler, E., Neale, F., Ponsford, M., Grinsell, L., *Earlier Medieval Sites (410-1066) in and around Bristol and Bath, the South Cotswolds and Mendip*,

Bristol Archaeological Research Group, 1980.

Godfrey, C.J., *The Church in Anglo-Saxon England*, Cambridge University Press, 1962.

Gomme, A., Jenner, M., and Little, B. *Bristol: An Architectural History*, Lund Humphries, 1979.

Good, G.L., *Some Aspects of the Development of the Redcliffe Waterfront in the Light of Excavation at Dundas Wharf*, in Bristol and Avon Archaeology 9, 1990/1, p.29- 42.

Good, G.L., *Excavation at Water Lane, by Temple Church, Bristol, 1971*, Bristol and Avon Archaeology 10, 1992, p.2-5.

Good, G.L., *Bristol Castle Keep: A Re-appraisal of the Evidence and Report on the Excavations in 1989*, Bristol and Avon Archaeology 13, 1996, p.17-45.

Graham-Campbell, J., *The Viking World*, Windward/Frances Lincoln, 1989.

Griffiths, O.M., *The Chapels of St Werburgha and St Blaise*, Transaction of the Bristol and Gloucestershire Archaeological Society, Vol.78, p.167-169, 1959.

Grinsell, L., *The Lower Bristol Avon as a Thoroughfare from Prehistoric Times to the Norman Conquest*, in Bristol and Avon Archaeology 5, 1986, p.2-4.

Hagen, A., *A Handbook of Anglo-Saxon Food, Processing and Consumption*, Anglo-Saxon Books, 1992.

Harris, W.L., *Filton, Gloucestershire, Some Account of the Village and Parish*, W.L. & L.N. Harris, 1995.

Hebditch, M., *Westbury College, Bristol*, in Bristol Archaeological Research Group Bulletin Vol.2, no.9, p.122.

Heighway, C., *Anglo-Saxon Gloucestershire*, Alan Sutton and Gloucestershire County Library, 1987.

Higham, R., and Barker, P., *Timber Castles*, B.T. Batsford, 1992.

Hill, D., *An Atlas of Anglo-Saxon England*, Basil Blackwell, 1984.

Hill, N., *St Nicholas Church, Whitchurch, Bristol*, privately printed, 1999.

Holt, J.C., *The Introduction of Knight Service in England*, in Strickland, M., ed. Anglo-Norman Warfare: Studies in Late Anglo-Saxon and Anglo-Norman Military Organization and Warfare, Boydell Press, 1992, p.41-58.

*Horfield Parish Church: A Brief History*, privately printed, 1996.

Horton, M., *Bristol and its International Position*, in Keene, L., 'Almost the Richest City', Bristol in the Middle Ages, Council for British Archaeology, 1997, p.9-17.

Iles, R., and Kidd, A., *Bristol: Jacob's Wells Road*, in Excavations in Bristol 1986-7, Bristol and Avon Archaeology 6, 1987, p.49.

Jones, R.H., and Burchill, R., *Excavations at St James' Priory, Bristol, 1988-9*, Bristol and Avon Archaeology 8, 1989, p.2-7.

Keen, L., ed. 'Almost the Richest City': Bristol in the Middle Ages, British Archaeological Association, 1997.

Kennett, D.H., *Ango-Saxon Pottery*, Shire Archaeology, 1989.

Kerr, M. & N., *Anglo-Saxon Architecture*, Shire Archaeology, 1983.

Knowles, D., and Hadcock, N., *Medieval Religious Houses in England and Wales*, Longman, 1971.

Knowles, D., *Westbury and the Benedictines*, in Norton, Rev. A.B., ed. *Westbury from 717 AD*, privately printed, 1999, p.6.

Laing, L., & J., *Anglo-Saxon England*, Granada, 1982.

Lapidge, M, Blair, J., Keynes, S. & Scragg, D., eds, *The Blackwell Encyclopedia of Anglo-Saxon England*, Blackwell, 1999.

Lawson, *Cnut: The Danes in England in the Early Eleventh Century*, Longman, 1993. Lindegaard, D. P., *Brislington Bulletins no.1, 1066 – 1600*, undated.

Lindley, E.S., *The Anglo-Saxon Charters of Stoke Bishop*, Transactions of the Bristol and Gloucestershire Archaeological Society, vol 78, 1959, p.97-109.

Linton, L., *Thornbury: Introduction*, in Bristol Archaeological Research Group Bulletin, Vol.4, no.8, Autumn 1973, p.222.

Lobel, M.D., and Carus-Wilson, E.M., *Historic Towns: Bristol*, The Scholar Press in association with the Historic Towns Trust, 1975.

Manco, J., *Iron Acton: A Saxon Nucleated Villlage*, in Transactions of the Bristol and Gloucestershire Archaeological Society 113, 1995, p.89-96.

MacInnes, C. M., & Whithead, W. F., eds, Bristol and its adjoining counties, Local Executive Committee of the British Association for the Advancement of Science, Bristol, 1955.

McGrath, P., and Cannon, J., eds, *Essays in Bristol and Gloucestershire History*, Centenary Volume of the Bristol and Gloucestershire Archaeological Society, 1976.

McGrath, P., ed, *The Religious Buildings of Keynsham*, Keynsham Civic Society, Saltford Local History Society and Allan Sutton Publishing, 1983.

Miguel, Maria Munoz de, *The Iconography of Christ Victor in Anglo-Saxon Art: A New Approach to the Study of the 'Harrowing of Hell' Relief in Bristol Cathedral*, in Keen, L., ed., 'Almost the Richest City': Bristol in the Middle Ages, British Archaeological Association, 1997, p.75-80.

Mills, A.D., *The Popular Dictionary of English Place Names*, Parragon Book Service Ltd, 1996.

Moore, J.S., *The Gloucestershire Section of Domesday Book: Geographical Problems of the Text*, part 2, Transactions of the Bristol and Gloucestershire Archaeological Society, Vol.106, 1988, p.7-106.

Neale, F., *Worship Street Bristol: A Puzzle Street-Name*, Bristol Archaeological Research Group Bulletin Vol.5, no.1, Spring 1974, p 6.

Nicholson, R.A., and Hillam, J., *A Dendrochronological Analysis of Oak Timbers from the Early Medieval Site at Dundas Wharf, Bristol*, Transactions of the Bristol and Gloucester-shire Archaeological Society, Vol.105, 1987, p.133-45.

Norton, A.B., *The Foundation of Westbury Church*, in *Westbury from 717 AD*, Norton, Rev. A.B., ed. privately printed, 1967, p.1-2.

Oakes, C., *Romanesque Architecture and Sculpture*, in Rogan, J. Canon, Bristol Cathedral: History and Architecture, Tempus, 2000, p.64-87.

Owen-Crocker, G.R., *Dress in Anglo-Saxon England*, Manchester University Press, 1986.

Phillips, Fr A., *The Hallowing of England: A Guide to the Saints of Old England and their Places of Pilgrimage*, Anglo-Saxon Books, 1994.

Ponsford, M.W., *Bristol Castle: Archaeology and the History of a Royal Fortress*, unpublished M Litt, dissertation, University of Bristol, 1979.

Ponsford, M.W., *Excavations at Westbury College, Bristol*, Bristol Archaeological Research Group Review 2, 1981, p.24-26.

Ponsford, M., Jones, R., Williams, B., Boore, E., Bryant, J., & Linge, A., *Archaeology in Bristol 1989*, Bristol and Avon Archaeology 8, 1989, p.41-5.

Ponsford, M., Good, L., Jones, R., Williams, B., Boore, E., Bryant, J., & Linge, A., *Archaeology in Bristol 1986-89*, Transactions of the Bristol and Gloucestershire archaeological Society vol.107, 1989, p.243-251.

Ponsford, M., Jones, R., Williams, B., Boore, E., Bryant, J., and Linge, A., Archaeology in Bristol 1989, Transactions of the Bristol and Gloucestershire Archaeological Society, Vol.108, 1990, p.175-83.

Price, D., *The Normans in Gloucestershire and Bristol*, 1983

Price, R., with Ponsford, M., *St Bartholomew's Hospital, Bristol: The Excavation of a Medieval Hospital 1976-8*, CBA Research Report 110, Council for British Archaeology, 1998.

Price, R., *Excavations at St Bartholomews Hospital, Bristol*, Bristol Archaeological Research Group Bulletin no.3, Winter, 1977, p.72-3.

Price, R., *Excavations at St Bartholomew's Hospital, Bristol, 1976-8*, Bristol Archaeological Research Group Bulletin no.5, Autumn 1978, p.123-5.

Pritchard, J.E., *The Pithay, Bristol, Norman Pottery and Wall*, Transactions of the Bristol and Gloucestershire Archaeological Society, Vol.48, 1926, p.251-74.

Rahtz, P.A., *Sub-Roman Cemeteries in Somerset*, Bristol Archaeological Research Group Bulletin, Vol.2, no.8, Autumn 1967, p.103-106.

Rhodes, J., *Money, Mints and Moneyers: Reflections on the Sylloge*, Bristol Archaeological Research Group Bulletin, Vol.5, no.1, Spring 1974.

Richards, J.D., *Viking Age England*, B.T. Batsford/English Heritage, 1991.

Rivet, A.L.F., and Smith, C., *The Place-Names of Roman Britain*, B.T. Batsford Ltd, 1979.

Rogan, Canon J., ed. Bristol Cathedral: History and Architecture, Tempus, 2000.

Ross, C.D., *Bristol in the Middle Ages*, in MacInnes, C. M., and Whitehead, W. F., eds, Bristol and Its Adjoining Counties, Local Executive Committee of the British Association for the Advancement of Science, Bristol, 1955.

Russell, J., *The Parish of Clifton*, Bristol Archaeological Research Group Bulletin, no.6, December 1978, p.138-143.

Russell, J., *The Archaeology of the Parish of Clifton with a Note on the 883 AD Boundary Survey of Stoke Bishop*, Bristol and Avon Archaeology, Vol.16, 1999, p.73-87.

Russell, J.R., and Williams, R.G.J., *Romano-British Sites in the City of Bristol: A Review and Gazetteer*, Bristol and Avon Archaeology 3, 1984, p.18-63.

Sanigar, W.T., *Leaves from a Barton Hill Notebook*, Bristol University, 1954.

Schofield, J., & Vince, A., *Medieval Towns*, Leicester University Press, 1994.

Sherborne, J.W., *The Port of Bristol in the Middle Ages*, The Bristol Branch of the Historical Association, Bristol University, 1987.

Smith, M. Q., *The Harrowing of Hell Relief in Bristol Cathedral*, Transactions of Bristol and Gloucestershire Archaeological Society, Vol 94, 1976, p.101-6.

Somerville-Large, P., *Dublin*, Hamish Hamilton, 1979.

Stenton, Sir F., *Anglo-Saxon England*, Oxford University Press, 1971.

Stewart, A., *An Anglo-Saxon Strap-End from Winterbourne, Bristol*, Bristol and Avon Archaeology 6, 1987, p 62.

Strickland, M., ed. *Anglo-Norman Warfare: Studies in Late Anglo-Saxon and Anglo-Norman Military Organisation and Warfare*, The Boydell Press, 1992.

Taylor, Rev. C.S., *Aust, The Place Of Meeting*, Transactions of the Bristol and Gloucestershire Archaeological Society, vol.24, 1901.

Todd, M., *The Northern Barbarians 100 BC - AD 300*, Basil Blackwell, 1987.

*Tower Lane, Watching Brief 1980-1*, Bristol and Avon Archaeology 1, 1982, p.53.

Tucker, S.I., *Anglo-Saxon Westbury*, in Westbury from 717 AD, Norton, Rev A.B., ed. privately printed, 1967, p.3-4.

Walker, D., *Bristol in the Early Middle Ages*, Bristol Branch of the Historical Association, University of Bristol, 1971.

Walker, D., *Gloucestershire Castles*, Transactions of the Bristol and Gloucestershire Archaeological Society, Vol.109, 1991, p.5-23.

Walker, M., *Old Somerset Customs*, Redcliffe Press Ltd, 1984.

Walker, R., *The Book of Almondsbury*, Barracuda Books, 1987.

Warner, P., *Sieges of the Middle Ages*, Barnes and Noble, 1968.

Watkins, M.J., *Gloucester, The Normans and Domesday – An Exhibition to Celebrated the 900th Anniversary of Domesday: Exhibition Catalogue and Guide*, Friends of Gloucester Museums, 1985.

Watts, L., & Rahtz, P., *Mary le Port, Bristol - Excavations 1962/3*, City of Bristol Museum and Art Gallery, 1985.

Welch, M., *Anglo-Saxon England*, B.T. Batsford/ English Heritage, 1992.

Whitelock, D., *The Pelican History of England: 2 The Beginnings of English Society*, Penguin Books, 1972.

Whittock, M., *Domesday Keynsham: Retrospective Examination of an Old English Royal Estate*, Bristol and Avon Archaeology 6, 1987, p.5-10.

Westbury College, in Westbury from 717 AD, Norton, Rev A.B., ed. privately printed, 1999.

Williams, A., *The English and the Norman Conquest*, Boydell and Brewer Ltd,1995.

Williams, B., *Excavations at Bristol Bridge, 1981*, Bristol and Avon Archaeology 1, 1982, p.12-15.

Williams, B., *St John's Street/Sheene Road, Bedminster*, in Archaeology in Bristol 1988-9, Bristol and Avon Archaeology Vol.7, 1989, p.33.

Williams, R.G.J., *Further Investigations at St John the Baptist Church, Bedminster*, in Bristol Archaeological Research Group Review, no.2, 1981, p.27-8.

Willis, T., *BARG Tour of Bristol Cathedral*, Bristol Archaeological Research Group Bulletin no.5, Autumn 1978, p.126-128.

Wilson, D.M., *The Anglo-Saxons*, Thames and Hudson, 1960.

Wormald, P., *Picture Essay 10 – The Burhs*, in Campbell, J., ed., The Anglo-Saxons, Penguin, 1982, p.152-3.

*Editorial review of Smith, A.H., The place-names of Gloucestershire*, English Place-Name Society, 1962, in BARG Bulletin Vol.1, no.1, Spring, 1962, p.103 Westbury's Saxon Grave Stone, in Westbury from AD717, in Norton, Rev A.B., ed., privately printed, 1999.

# Index